Channel
HO

Shoppir
Dieppe,

© 2000 by Passport Guide Publications
19 Morley Crescent, Edgware
Middlesex HA8 8XE

Written By: Sharron Livingston
Published By: Passport Guide Publications
Enquiries :   Tel: 020 8905 4851
Email: Sharron@channelhoppers.net
Web site: www.channelhoppers.net

Advertising   Tony Logie
Enquiries: Logie Bradshaw Media Ltd
          Tel: 01442 233331
          Fax: 01442 231131

All rights reserved.
No part of this publication may be reproduced, stored in a retrieval system or transmitted in
any form or by any means, electronic, mechanical, photocopying, recording, or otherwise or
used in any form of advertising, sales promotion or publicity without the prior permission of
Passport Guide Publications.

Notice:
Every effort has been made to ensure that this book contains accurate and current information
at the time of going to print. We cannot be liable for any subsequent changes.

ISBN: 09524319 7 1

Contents

Contents

Introduction

Think of Normandy and images of World War II may spring to mind. The Americans, English, Canadians and members of the allied forces still solemnly commiserate the tragedy of D-Day. Normandy itself has ensured, through many memorial sites, that the tragedies of war are never forgotten especially as much of the Normandy coast had to be entirely rebuilt. In fact its turbulent history records wars, plagues and invasions dating as far back as the Viking landings in Dieppe. Nothing is forgotten and everything can be remembered or learned at any of the numerous memorials or museums throughout Normandy.

Post-war reconstruction has now been achieved and tourists can enjoy Normandy for its brilliant culture, its gastronomy, its architecture and customs.

Think of Normandy again and let images of apples, cider, calvados, cheese, timbered houses, dovecots, awesome cliffs and impressive abbeys appear before the mind's eye.

Normandy is divided into two administrative regions: Upper Normandy and Lower Normandy. The raison d'être of this book is to guide you through the main areas of the Seine-Maritime department of Upper Normandy. In particular, the port of Dieppe, Rouen - the administrative capital - and the port of Le Havre.

Within this triangular area, you can savour the history, enjoy the fabulous stretch of coastal scenery and still get a good dose of retail therapy. Our researchers have lovingly pinpointed the best restaurants, hotels and shops and also managed to negotiate some special offers for Channel Hoppers. **Enjoy!**

Enjoy peace of mind cover at home and abroad

with Green Flag European Services

Did you know that **Green Flag** offers an extensive range of European Services to bring you peace of mind throughout your visit to Europe?

As well as offering an exceptional UK vehicle rescue service to its 4 million members, **Green Flag** offers a comprehensive range of motoring and travel-related European Services to both members and non-members.

The following services are available to non-members:

European Motoring Assistance

Our European Motoring Assistance package brings you complete peace of mind in the event of a breakdown, accident, fire or theft whilst abroad. It includes passenger and vehicle repatriation if needed.

European Travel Insurance

Our policy brings you cover for a variety of situations including injury, cancellation of your holiday, theft of your property, additional accommodation costs and legal expenses.

Ferry and Eurotunnel Booking Service

Green Flag can help you with your travel plans by booking your channel crossing at a time which fits in with your travel plans. We also offer valuable discounts on selected ferry crossings and our experienced operators can offer helpful advice.

All **Green Flag** European Services offer high standards at great value for money prices. So next time you're planning a visit to Europe, give us a call.

Call European Services FREE
0800 400 638

Green Flag
Motoring Assistance

Hopping Over

Cross-Channel hopping has become a familiar way of life for many in recent years. The attractions are obvious; it makes an easy and inexpensive short break abroad, there are very real bargains to be had in food, wine, beer and spirits, the chance to savour excellent French meals in the huge variety of cafés, restaurants, bistros and brasseries - and, last but not least, the many things to do and places to see within a short drive of the ports.

How to Book Your Next Trip

One of the best specialist tour operators offering short breaks across the channel is Great Escapes, part of the Allez France group.

Their range of excellent value short breaks are fully inclusive of travel, accommodation, information and those little "extras" that make the trip so much more enjoyable. Examples include their three-day, two-night break to Champagne, starting at only £69, including cross-Channel travel with your car, 3-star hotel accommodation, breakfasts, a "Champagne Tourist Route" guidebook, map, a free bottle of Champagne in your hotel room, and a free tour and tasting at the cellars of one of the top-name Champagne houses.

Other Great Escapes breaks include: Le Touquet, Chateaux and Manor Houses, Budget France, Bruges, Lille, Honfleur, Brussels, Antwerp, Paris and more.

Hopping Over

How to Cross

Great Escapes (FREEphone 0800 198 1199) offer all the most convenient Channel crossings within their range of short breaks. The options (by car) are:

Hoverspeed - the fastest way to cross by sea. Hoverspeed operate three types of stylish fast craft: the famous Hovercraft ply the Dover-Calais route in only 35 minutes, the SeaCat links Folkestone & Boulogne in 55 minutes (33% faster than any ferry),and Dover to Ostend in under two hours (Ostend is just 16 miles from Bruges!) and the SuperSeaCat crosses the Channel at 40mph from Newhaven to Dieppe in just over two hours. First Class seats are available through Great Escapes at a small supplement, giving you priority boarding, a hot towel, and tasty snacks served on china crockery.

Eurotunnel - Drive on, drive off "Shuttle" trains (up to 4 an hour at peak times). A smooth, fast 35 minute crossing whatever the weather! Join straight from the M20, and drive off straight onto the Calais-Boulogne autoroute.

P & O Stena Line - operate large conventional "superferries" from Dover to Calais. The vessels have extensive on-board facilities including cafés, play areas, bars, lounges, etc. There is usually a sailing every hour during the day. Crossing time is 75 minutes.

For information, reservations or a
"Great Escapes" brochure,
call FREEphone 0800 198 1199

Hopping Over

The perks of shopping abroad start on board where products are available at low French duty paid prices once the vessel has reached French territorial waters.

From	To	Company	Crossing Time	Frequency
Folkestone	Calais Coquelles	**Eurotunnel** Tel: 0990 353 535 No foot passengers Check in: 30 mins	35 mins	Every 15 minutes
Dover	Calais Port	**Hoverspeed** Tel: 0870 240 241 Check in: 20 mins	35mins	Hourly
		P&O Stena Line Tel: 0990 980 980 Check in: 30 mins	75mins	every 45 mins at peak time
		SeaFrance Tel: 0990 711 711 Check in: 45 mins	90 mins	Every 90 mins at peak time
Folkestone	Boulogne	**Hoverspeed** Tel: 0870 240 241 Check in: 30 mins	55 mins	Hourly peak time
Newhaven	Dieppe	**Hoverspeed** Tel 0870 240 241 Check in: 30 mins	2hr 15mins	2/3 daily seasonal
Portsmouth	Le Havre	**P&O Portsmouth** Tel: 0870 2424 999 Check in: 30 mins	5hr 30mins	3 daily

Hopping Over

It may be convenient to start your journey from Dover or Folkestone. Driving to Normandy from Calais or Boulogne is easy thanks to good road networks.

From/to	Miles approx
Calais/Boulogne	40
Calais/Dieppe	107
Calais/Le Havre	172
Calais/Rouen	115
Dieppe/Le Havre	65
Dieppe/ Rouen	60
Le Havre/Rouen	54

From Calais to Dieppe
Take the A16 motorway or the scenic D940 coastal road. Start on the A16 then divert onto the D940 at Abbeville towards Treport. At Treport switch to the D925. Allow 2.5 hours (less 20 minutes if your are starting at Boulogne).

From Calais to Rouen
Take the A16 motorway and then the A28 direct to Rouen - Allow 3 hours for your journey.

From Dieppe to Rouen
Take the N27 all the way. - Allow 1 hour for your journey.

From Le Havre to Rouen
Take the N15 all the way - Allow 1.5 hours for the journey.

How Do You Say?

It's amazing how a few choice French phrases will break the ice with the locals and greatly enhance your enjoyment.

Pleasantries

Nice to meet you	Enchanté
Yes/No	Oui/non
Good Morning/Good Day	Bonjour
How are you?	Ça va
Good Evening/ Night/ Bye	Bonsoir/bonne nuit/Au revoir
Excuse me	Excusez-moi
Thank you / You're welcome	Merci / Je vous en prie

Being Understood

I don't speak French	Je ne parle pas français
I don't understand	Je ne comprends pas
Do you speak English?	Parlez-vous anglais?
I don't know how to say it in French	Je ne sais pas le dire en français

Eating Out

A table for two please	Une table pour deux, s'il vous plaît
The menu please	Le menu, s'il vous plaît
Do you have a children's menu?	Avez-vous un menu pour les enfants?
We'll take the set menu, please	Nous prendrons le menu, s'il vous plaît
We would like a dessert	Nous aimerions du dessert
The bill please	L'addition, s'il vous plaît
Is service included?	Le service est compris?
Do you accept credit cards?	Acceptez-vous les cartes de crédit?

Hotels

I'd like a single/double room	Je voudrais une chambre pour une personne/deux personnes
I reserved a room in the name of:	J'ai réservé un chambre au nom de:
I confirmed my booking by phone/letter	J'ai confirmé ma réservation par téléphone/lettre
My key, please	Ma clé, s'il vous plaît
What time is breakfast/dinner?	Le petit déjeuner/Le dîner est à quelle heure?
I shall be leaving tomorrow	Je partirai demain

Paying

How much is it?	Ça coûte Combien?
I'd like to pay please	On veut payer, s'il vous plaît
Can I have the bill please?	L'addition, s'il vous plaît
Can I pay by credit card?	Puis-je payer avec une carte de credit?
Do you accept traveller's cheques/ Eurocheques/Sterling?	Acceptez-vous les cheques de voyages/Eurocheques/Sterling?

Speak French? Speak It Better With

Champs-Elysées ®

LA FRANCE EN CD ET CASSETTE

Join the thousands of intermediate and advanced students of French who use *Champs-Elysées* to maintain or improve their fluency. The international audiomagazine for people who love France and the French language, *Champs-Elysées* is produced monthly in Paris by top-notch French broadcasters and journalists. Each hour-long cassette or CD brings you interviews and conversation about a variety of topics, including current events, gastronomy, the arts, and travel. A word-for-word transcript comes with each edition, complete with an extensive French-English glossary and informative background notes. Study supplements, priced separately, help build listening comprehension with exercises based on selected programme segments.

TO ORDER, CALL
0800 833 257

"In a word—excellent. Very polished and professional...a very good buy...Strongly recommended."
—*The Journal of the Association for Language Learning (UK)*

MONEY-BACK GUARANTEE

YES, *Please rush me my first audiomagazine!*

☐ 5 monthly editions (£55) ☐ On CD, add £17.50 ☐ Supplement, add £15
☐ 11 monthly editions (£99) ☐ On CD, add £38.50 ☐ Supplement, add £33

Price is inclusive of P&P.

Name _____

Address _____

☐ Cheque enclosed. Please debit my ☐ VISA ☐ MasterCard ☐ American Express ☐ Eurocard ☐ Switch ☐ Diners

Card no _____ Expiry _____ Signed _____

For faster service, order with your credit card via telephone: 0800 833 257 or FAX to 0117 929 2426
Outside the UK call (44) 117 929 2320 • To order online, go to *http://ads.champs-elysees.com/CHG1*

POST TO: CHAMPS-ELYSEES, DEPT. CHG1, FREEPOST LON 295, BRISTOL, BS1 6FA

Dieppe is the oldest and some say, the prettiest of the French ports. It has even been referred to as 'The Brighton of France'

This pretty, one thousand year old ancient town, nestling in a basin surrounded by the cliffs of the Alabaster* coast, is famed for its now defunct ivory trade, and equally for being the third largest scallop fishing port in France. In fact, the St Jacques scallops are known world-wide. So profound is its link to fishing, that even in 1030, the abbey of Mont Ste-Catherine-de-Rouen rented the area for 5000 smoked herrings.

The word Dieppe literally means 'deep'. It was referred to as 'djupa' by the Vikings who found the inshore waters deep and safe and therefore the best place to land their boats. This established Dieppe as a harbour and by the 16th century it had become the major port of the Kingdom of France. Like most of Northern France, Dieppe suffered great human losses during WWII. In the spring of 1942 Dieppe had to undergo a major raid in the hope of weakening the German hold on the area and achieve the liberation of Europe. Unfortunately, the Germans were more than ready and the operation code named 'Operation Jubilee', became a controversial bone of contention, some claiming it was a tragic blunder with 5,000 Canadian soldiers lost within two hours. Others bestowed upon the tragedy a sense of strategy in that it allowed an invasion of the continent. A memorial Canadian cemetery is attached to the Château museum and can be visited.

Dieppe

Dieppe no longer holds out its welcome mat to the ferries as they have ceased travelling this route. The old harbour at **Quai Henri VI** is still lined with a veritable choice of seafood restaurants but the view now is of moored

stairway to heaven - and Normandy my gateway to Paradise'.

The new port, however, is still, to the relief of the hotels and shopkeepers in Dieppe, frequented by the superfast SeaCat.

Dieppe Harbour

yachts and a busy car park rather than marine activity. The politician, Denis Healey, very much advocated keeping the Newhaven to Dieppe line open. In 1998 he is quoted as romanticising the route:
"Since the first time I crossed the Channel, in 1936 as a student, the ferry from Newhaven has been my

Dieppe's fine pebble beach is over a mile long and is set back from the shore. It provides a huge expanse of lawn and play areas ideal for the kids. Those who are not afraid of the cold can do as the Duchesse de Barry did in 1806. She, in effect, started the skinny dipping fad by encouraging her aristocratic friends to immerse themselves in the chilly though refreshing waters at the sandy western end.

Pretty this port may be, but ironically Dieppe offers little in the way of sight-seeing interest. Nevertheless, a good walk-about is highly recommended for three reasons. Firstly, the one way road system is highly infuriating to the uninitiated driver and secondly, the beach, the shopping and the gastronomy can only be truly appreciated on foot. Lastly, everything in Dieppe is within walking distance. The beach, the port and all the places of interest are actually within the heart of town.

For instance, overlooking the beach and perched on top of a hill, is the **Château museum**. If you climb up, you will have a fabulous view of Dieppe as well as benefiting from the cultural offerings of the museum. On the end of the cliff above the castle is the **Panorama.** The view takes in several small rivers and the surrounding steep cliff.

Whilst on foot, take a walk around the quaint pedestrianised centre. On Saturday mornings a pulsating open-air market emerges in the large

square at the foot of the **Grande Rue** in **Place National**. Trading spills over into **rue St Jacques** and **rue St Jean** with local and not so local farmers selling an array of edible wares produced on their farms. Products include French cheese, sausages, olives and honey from Provence.

On display in **Place Nationale** is the statue of **Duquesne** who beat the invincible Rutyer in 1676. He was a devout Protestant and despite his obvious military prowess and achievement, he was refused promotion from Lieutenant General to Admiral of the French fleet because he would not renounce his faith.

Along the **Grande Rue** and its charming side streets you will find a bounty of idiosyncratic boutiques, various restaurants and specialist shops. It is hard to imagine that our Gallic ancestors had to wade through marshland to get from one end of this road to the other because at that time the Grande Rue was submerged under high tides.

When you get to the Chemist look out for the plaque with the name **Descroisilles**. In a way this one man changed the lives of many forever by inventing the coffee filter.

If it is raining though, hop back into the car and take the **Rouen road** to the **Belvedere** indoor shopping centre where parking is not a problem. It has 55 shops including Auchan hypermarket and for those with a taste for fast food, Macdonalds.

Remarkably, Dieppe is said to have over a hundred eating places. Why remarkable? The population is a mere 36,000 and that equates to one restaurant for every 360 residents!

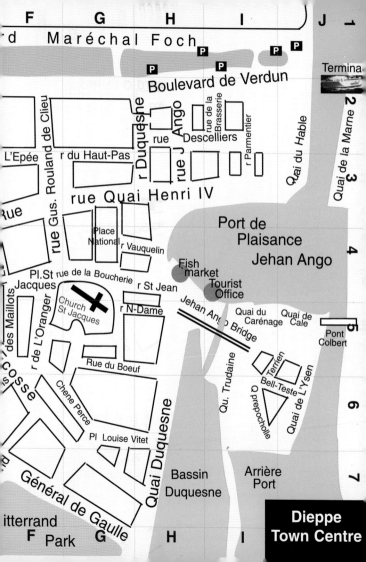

Dieppe Town Centre

Musée du Château
Castle Museum
rue de Chastes

17th century Dieppe saw a speciality craft in carved ivory. This medieval castle, which looms over the west end of the town, is home to a collection of these ivories. There are also paintings by Renoir, Boudin, Pissarro and Braque together with archeological pieces found in the region. Maritime objects on display include model ships and navigational instruments.
Tel: 00 33 (0)2 35 84 19 76

Castle Museum of Dieppe

Open daily
June 1st-September 30th
10am-12am & 2pm-6pm
October 1st-May 31st
10am-12am & 2pm-5pm
(6pm on Sunday)
Closed Tuesdays

Closed: 1 January, 1 May, 1 November, 31 December

Tel: 02 35 84 19 76
Fax: 02 32 90 12 79
www.mairie-dieppe.fr

The Square du Canada
A flight of stairs from the Musée du Château leads to this square. Sailors from Dieppe who played a role in the country's colonisation are commemorated here. Equally, it commemorates more than 3000 Canadian casualties claimed by the disastrous allied commando raid that took place in Dieppe in 1942 - a series of suicidal landings and attacks up sheer and well defended cliff faces. Some soldiers were killed even before they could touch ground.

The Ivory & Spice Route

The ivory and spice trade started six hundred years ago when two ships returned to Dieppe from West Africa with a cargo of ivory and spices. It became a major import trade for Dieppe. The trade no longer exists but there is an ivory and spice trail for those interested in learning more.

The route starts at Dieppe with the Musée du Château and then heads for Etretat, looping inland to the château at Bailleul, Valmont, Cany-Barville, Galleville , Miromesnil, the ruined feudal castle of Arques-la-Bataille and then back to Dieppe.

In the 17th century there were 350 ivory carvers in Dieppe. There are only two now where you can buy pieces of carved ivory. Both craftsmen are located in the Rue Ango.

St Jacques Church
rue St Jacques

The towering 14th century church of St Jacques, is the only high rise structure left in Dieppe. It is a stunning mix of Flamboyant and Renaissance styles. Its fan of chapels and the majestic tower were added later in the 16th century during the Hundred Years' War. Inside there is a wall of the treasury known as the 'frieze of the savages'.

The artist Camille Pissaro had a good view of the church from his hotel window at the Hotel du Commerce at Place Nationale. He was so inspired he painted eight variations of the church.

The 17th century buildings in narrow streets of St Jacques' Quarter behind the church replaced those burned down in the 1694.

Dieppe Sights

Active Leisure

Horse Riding
Centre Equestre du
Cheval bleu,
Bellengreville
at the foot of the forest of
Arcques.
Tel:00 33 (0)235 85 76 21

Golf
Golf de Dieppe - 18 hole
Route de Pourville
Tel:00 33 (0)235 84 25 05
Golf clubs can be hired

Fishing
Fish from jetties for
conger eels in autumn
and bass from Berneval
beach and from boats for
cod. Boat hire:
Tel: 00 33 (0)235 84 90 98

Beach Front

Wind Surfing
This is popular among
enthusiasts and facilities
are available.

Play Area
Secure play area and
games for kids.

St Rémy Church
Rue du 10 Août 1942
St Rémy church was built
between 1522 and 1645.
Unfortunately, it was used
as an arms dump by the
Germans and was blown
up just one day before the
town was liberated in 1944.
It is now known for its fine
18th century Parisot and
Paul organ, its stained
glass windows from Sèvres
and Lusson and its Louis
XIII-style facade.

Cité de la Mer
rue de L'Asile Thomas

This exhibition depicts the
history of ship-building,
techniques used by the
fishing industry, sea life and
geology unique to the
Seine-Maritime area. The
guided tour includes a
smoked herring snack and
ends with a visit to the
small but relaxing
aquarium. Admission: FF38
Tel: 00 33 2 35 06 20
Further details also from: email:
Estran.CiteDeLaMer@wanadoo.fr

Café des Tribunaux
place Puits Salé

The 18th century Café des Tribunaux is the oldest pub in Dieppe. It used to be the local hang-out for Oscar Wilde where he allegedly wrote 'the Ballad of Reading Goal'. The artists of the day, Pissaro, Renoir, Monet, Sickert also spent much time here.

Apparently, during an encounter here, the painter Walter Sickert reputedly advised Paul Gauguin to give up art and remain a bank clerk! These days the clientele and atmosphere is somewhat different, but a visit is almost obligatory. In front of the Café is a salt water well.

Puits Salé

-

Salt water well in front of the Tribunaux Café

Tourist Office
Pont Jehan Ango
quai de Carénage
Tel:00 33 (0)235 84 11 77
In the summer, the tourist office sprawls out along the beach everyday between 10am-7.30 to ease the congestion.

Petit Train
The train makes a one-hour narrated tour of Dieppe. It starts at the tourist office and heads to the Cité de la Mer, then back along the beach. There are 8 journies daily between 8am and 5pm. Tariff FF35

How to get from the Port to the Town

At the roundabout take the third exit. Continue over the second roundabout. At the third roundabout take the first exit, past the racecourse to the next roundabout. This will bring you to the town centre.

Le Quartier du Pollet
A Walk About
Le Pollet and the cliff

For more than 1000 years and to this day, the picturesque district of Le Pollet with its small alleyways, petite cottages, and red brick buildings, has been the fishermans' quarter. This eastern suburb is distinguishable too by a certain Italian flavour. When ships called in from Venice on their way to Flanders the locals were influenced by their Italian visitors. The Polletais betray their Italian link with their speech and even with their mannerisms.

To enjoy a peaceful walk around the area, cross over the **Pont (**bridge of) **Jehan Ango.** The bridge separates the ferry port from the **Port de Pêche** (fishing port) and acts as a link to the Pollet. Once across, follow the **Quai du Carénage** and cross over the largest rotating bridge in France - the **Colbert bridge** - built in 1889. Turn into the **rueille des Grèves**. The butcher's shop situated there has a 19th century statue of Our Lady of the Strands which is the remains of a former chapel on the site. At **rue Guerrier** take a right and after number 24 you will see the old and picturesque **rue Quiquengrogne** - a strange word which was the battle cry of the Channel pirates in the 15th century.

Turn back along rue Guerrier and after number 34 turn into the **rue du Petit-Fort** to number 3. This is a tiny uninhabited fisherman's house with a collapsed roof, built before the 1694 English bombardment.

At the top of the street climb the steps on the right to get to the cliff top and to the **Notre-Dame de Bon Secours** church. The church was built in 1876 in memory of those lost at sea. From here the views of land and sea, the beach and the town's rooftops are magnificent.

Shopping in Dieppe

Auchan
Belvedere Shopping
Centre
Tel: 00 33 (0)235

Bus: Take the courtesy bus from the terminal to the town centre. Walk two minutes to the tourist office and catch Bus number 2 or 22 direct to Auchan,

English: No

Tasting: No

Payment:

Parking:

Open: 8.30am to 10pm

Closed: Sunday

How To Get There

From the terminal turn right (2nd exit at roundabout). Continue over the next two roundabouts, passing the racecourse on the left. At the next roundabout take the 3rd exit. Belevedere Shopping Centre is perched on the left of the following roundabout (3rd exit) on the Rouen road.

Auchan Hypermarket's French wine range is very extensive, in that it includes 150 differently labelled wines from all the French regions. Augmenting the range are a further 70 or so sparkling wines such as Champagne in the higher price bracket, to Pol Remy which at just FF7 a bottle has enough fizz to go down well at any teenage party.   Also on the shelves are a range of 45 wines from other countries, and these are generally supplied by Sainsbury's, the most famous being Jacob's Creek carrying a price tag of FF30.

Auchan is probably the best place in Dieppe to buy beers, where the range includes Belgium and Continental beers. Auchan is also favoured for its spirits. Other products such as Coke are also good value with a 2 litre bottle costing less than £1 at FF8.70.

Shopping in Dieppe

What's on offer At Auchan - A Selection

Prices converted here for your convenience at an exchange rage of FF10 to £1.

Champagne		FF	£
Alfred Rothschild		98.00	9.80
Mercier		101.60	10.16
Lanson		118.01	11.81
Piper Heidsick		128.60	12.86
Mumm cordon Rouge		129.15	12.92
Moët et Chandon		141.30	14.13
Laurent Perrier		142.05	14.25
Veuve Clicquot Ponsardin		149.75	14.98
Beers	%	FF	£
Munsterbrau 10 x 25cl	4.7	13.45	1.35
Guinness 6 x 33cl	4.2	35.65	3.57
Sterling 25 x 25cl	4.9	35.95	3.60
1664 12 x 25cl	5.9	36.30	3.63
St Omer 24 x 25cl	5.0	40.61	4.61
33 Export	4.8	42.95	4.30
Kanterbrau 24 x 25cl	4.5	43.55	4.36
Pelforth 20 x 25cl	5.8	44.97	4.50
Stella Artois 24 x 25 cl	5.2	48.85	4.85
Spirits	%	FF	£
Cinzanno Bianco & Rosso 1L	14.0	40.95	4.95
Dubonnet 1L	16.0	46.06	4.67
Sandeman port 75cl	19.0	50.03	5.03
Noilly Prat 1L	18.0	53.05	5.31
Martini Extra Dry 1L	18.0	54.49	5.50
Gordons Gin 70cl	37.5	67.05	6.71
Grants 70cl	40.0	69.75	6.98
Smirnoff 7cl	37.5	70.05	7.05
Teachers 70cl	40.0	80.90	8.90
Absolute Vodka 70cl	40.0	84.90	8.49
Tia Maria 7cl	26.5	104.68	10.47
Bombay Sapphire 70cl	40.0	105.55	10.56
Grand Marnier 70cl	40.0	106.76	10.68
Glenfiddich 70cl	40.0	127.09	12.71
Chivas Regal 12 yrs 70cl	40.0	144.29	14.43
Benedictine 70cl	40.0	161.65	16.17
Glenmorangie 70cl	40.0	170.25	17.25
Remy Martin 70cl	40.0	172.35	17.24

Shopping in Dieppe

L'Epicier Olivier
18 rue St Jacques
76200 Dieppe
Tel: 00 33 (0)235 84 22 55

English: Some
Tasting: Yes
Payment: [cards]
Parking: Not easily
Closed: Sunday & Monday

How To Get There
Park your car along the seafront (Blvd de Verdun. Turn into quai Duquesne, 2nd right into Grande Rue. Take 3rd left into rue des Maillots, then right into rue St Jacques.

Fine food, cheese, coffee and wine are all prized in France, equally by the French who take them for granted and by the visitor seeking a gastronomic adventure. To find this combination of products under one roof, a discerning shopper should visit an epicerie.

A good example is the L'épicerie Olivier. Monsieur Olivier has been trading for some 40 years offering Norwegian smoked salmon, a variety of 100 French cheeses, including the popular Norman Neufchâtel, fois gras and of course wines. The range of 300 medium priced wines are all French (with some emphasis on Bordeaux) and are sold under the Nicholas banner.

Special Offer
The smell of roasted coffee may ignite some epicurean lust. If so, show your guide and Monsieur Olivier will be happy to offer you a free tasting of his wines and cheeses.

25

Shopping in Dieppe

The Hoverstore
Hoverspeed
76200 Dieppe

English: Yes
Tasting: No
Payment: £, Major currencies

Parking: Yes
Open: Daily

If you would like to buy your wine from a popular international range of good value wines then the Hoverstore is the place to stock up.

The range includes the eternal best seller, Liebfraumilch at just 99p as well as famous Australian offerings such as Oxford Landing at £3.50, Jacob's Creek at £2.90, Penfolds at £3.25 and Nottage Hill Chardonnay 1999 at £3.00. Famous Champagnes are on offer but if you wish to try something different, the

How To Get There
Check-in on your way home to gain access to the shop.

Gardet Cuvée St Flavy looks incredible value at £8.80 a bottle.

Hoverspeed have made buying very easy for foot passengers with their Select & Collect scheme. The idea is that you make and pay for your selection in the continental Hoverstore and then take your purchases to the Select & Collect loading point. Your purchases will be waiting for you on your return to the UK port.

Special Offer

Spend £20 and receive a
FREE
bottle of house wine

Offer limited to 1 per person on presentation of of The Channel Hopper's Guide

Shopping in Dieppe

Michel Pommier
22-24 place National
76200 Dieppe
Tel: 00 33 (0)235 84 14 62

English: Yes
Tasting: No
Payment: £, 💳 💳

Parking: Yes
Open: 9am-12.15p &
2pm-7.3pm daily
Sun 10am-noon

How To Get There

Park your car along the seafront (Blvd de Verdun. Turn into quai Duquesne, 2nd right into Grande Rue. Take 1st left. The shop is on the corner of Grande rue and place National.

An unusual outlet which you will stumble across by merely following your nose. The aroma of roasted coffee is most alluring, and the coffee display dominates the entrance. Monsieur Pommier roasts ten varieties on the premises. There is also a range of teas, which the British seem to enjoy buying. Also on display are a range of chocolates.

The wines are, as is typical of French outlets, entirely French, and the range is made up of mostly fine, quality wines. A range of whiskys and liqueurs are available too.

Even if you find the wines a tad expensive, this is still a nice shop to visit.

Shopping in Dieppe

Le Sommelier
27 rue des Maillots
76200 Dieppe
Tel: 00 33 (0)235 06 05 20

English: Yes
Tasting: Yes
Payment: £, Major currencies

Parking: Yes
Open: 9.30am to 12 noon &
            2pm to 7pm
Closed: Monday

How To Get There

Park your car along the seafront (Blvd de Verdun. Turn into quai Duquesne, 2nd right into Grande Rue. Take 3rd left into rue des Maillots.

The word sommelier can be loosely translated as a 'wine butler', and this is how the proprietor of this outlet, Monsieur Boudard Jean-Marie describes himself.

The six year old outlet is pleasantly crammed full of 'fine' wines (all French of course) - 620 of them to be precise. The selection includes wines from all the French regions and in particular Bordeaux, Beaujolais, Rhône, Loire and Burgundy. The Champagne selection looks pretty good too.

Special Offer

10% off

all your purchases when you show your Channel Hopper's Guide.

What is Belvedere?

Belvédère Shopping Centre

Avenue des Canadiens
76200 Dieppe

Bus: No 2. Catch it outside the tourist office.
Parking: Yes
Open: 10am to 8pm daily
Closed: Sunday

Just outside Dieppe, perched on the Rouen Road is the modern Belvédère indoor shopping centre. On a rainy day, this shopping centre is an ideal alternative.

Unlike shops within Dieppe centre, shopping does not have to stop for lunch here as the outlets stay open throughout the day. And of course parking is far easier. What you do miss out on, however, is the opportunity to do your shoping in typically French outlets.

There are 58 outlets in total

How To Get There

From the terminal turn right (2nd exit at roundabout). Continue over the next two roundabouts, passing the racecourse on the left. At the next roundabout take the 3rd exit. Belvédère Shopping Centre is perched on the left of the following roundabout (3rd exit) on the Rouen road.

and these include Auchan hypermarket where you can stock up on beer and wine, sports shops, gift shops, and a series of French fashion stores. The eateries tend to be familiar fast food restaurants such as McDonalds, Quick and Flunch. Conveniently though, there is also petrol station where the prices are marginally cheaper than elsewhere.

Take the spectacular coastal road from Dieppe to Le Havre (or the other way round) and enjoy the beauty and the sights of the various resorts of the 70 or so miles on this stretch of the Alabaster Coast along the

way. Known as the Caux country, the road of this massive chalk plateau runs alongside the English Channel to Etretat. The last 13 miles towards Le Havre snake a little more inland running through picturesque farmland.

From Dieppe pick up the D75 at rue **Faubourg de la Barre** in the direction of **St Valéry-en-Caux**. The first resort, 3km later, is **Pourville-sur-mer**, a very peaceful bay with

just a handful of hotels and other miscellaneous buildings. Further on route take in the wonderful sea views while passing through **Varengeville-sur-Mer.** The coastal road here is a wooded collection of townships which together constitute Varengeville. It has just 1000 inhabitants but artists such as Monet and Dufy spent time here. The parents of the British prime minster, Anthony Eden, were born here and Jean Ango, a shipbuilder cum politician, had his summer palace, **Manoir d'Ango,** built in the area in 1530.  It is an example of exceptional Italian Renaissance architecture and within its quadrangle there is an impressive dovecote. He filled the palace with busts of the great and the good - including himself. Access is via a track off to the left but you can only view the exterior of the building.

Close to the coast on the cliffs of Varengeville is the flower garden of **Parc Floral du Bois des Moutiers.** The garden is based on an 18th century English garden design. Both the house and its gardens were created in 1898 by Sir E. Lutyens, G. Jeckell and G. Mallet Among the floral display It features rhododendrons, azaleas, magnolias and an array of spring time shrubs. The park situated alongside the gardens sprawls right out to the sea. The Parc Floral du Bois des Moutiers is open from March to November but admission is fairly expensive at FF40. Tel: 00 33 32 35 85 10 02.

The town's church, **St Valéry,** is situated on the cliff top and stands at the centre of the town's cemetery. In its south choir aisle it has a bewitching stained glass **Tree of Jesse** by Georges Braque, a cubist painter who lived here in 1930. As the road loops through a most beautiful landscape, it passes by the beaches of **Ste-Marguerite sur Mer**, **St Aubin sur Mer.**

As the road heads towards **Sotteville sur Mer**, it changes to the D68. To take a dip in the beach at the pleasant village resort of **Sotteville** you will have to contend with some 250 steps.

Following the coast will lead you to **Veules-les Roses**, - a pretty name for a pretty resort almost hidden by the wooded cliffs. The area at **Veules-les Roses** is known by the local tourist office as a 'mini-Venice' as it is situated by the smallest river in France The **Veules**. The **Veules** is just 1,100 metres long and it flows into the sea after winding its way around thatched roofed houses and windmills. This area is also known for its fine pebble beach and pretty back gardens.

Whilst here visit the **Château et Roseraie du Mesnil-Geoffroy.** It has a fabulous maze and boasts over 1800 different types of roses.

Turn right onto the D925 which sweeps into **Saint-Valery-en Caux.** This busy port has 5000 inhabitants and is a popular centre for sailors stopping off to stock up before continuing their voyage. It is also one of the few resorts which stays lively throughout the year, even in the winter

months. The marvellous timbered renaissance house, **Maison Henri IV**, that you can spot from the quay has the dual purpose of being the tourist office and an art gallery. Behind it is a picturesque alley leading to the old 17th century convent of the Penitents, currently used as a hospital.

Onwards on the D925 towards **Fécamp** and turn on to the D68 in the direction of **St Sylvain**. Then over the flat landscape into **St Martin aux Buneaux** and to **Sassetot-le-Mauconduit**. Look out for the huge **Château de Sassetot**. Before it was converted into a hotel-restaurant, this beautiful chateau was once the home of the Austrian Empress, Sissi who lived there in 1875.

Continue onto the D150. The road which leads to the remains of the **Abbaye de Valmont**. **Valmont** is connected to the sea by dense forests of the **Vallemont.** It was once the feudal stronghold of the Estouteville family. Nicolas d'Estouteville founded the Benedictine abbey in 1169. The 15th century windows depict the life of the Virgin Mary. The ruins of the flint and brick church is in the centre of the town at the foot of the copse.

Follow the leisurely flow of the sea along the D150 for 11km and you will be in **Fécamp.**

The view of the cliffs from the promenade at Fécamp

Tourist Offices

Saint Valery en Caux
Maison Henri IV
Saint Valery en Caux
Tel:00 33 (0)35 97 00 63

Veules les Roses
Rue du Marché
76980 Vueles les Roses
Tel:00 33 (0)235 83 54 64

The history of this trendy seaside resort is imbued with images of the 'Precious Blood of Christ' and Benedictine liqueur

Fécamp is a most agreeable seaside resort adorned with an inviting beach and magnificent cliffs. But as well as beauty the port also benefits from the bustle of being a main market town and an important cod-fishing port. Just as important however, are its historical, and religious roots. In fact at one time Fécamp was a greater medieval pilgrimage site than even its famous successor at Mont-St-Michel.

As is usual in France, Fécamp has its own selection of churches, duchys, palaces and museums.

Eglise De La Trinité
23 rue des Forts

This church, one of the largest in France, is symbolic of the prestige of Fécamp, the capital of the dukes of Normandy. Fécamp's religious routes are based at the convent dedicated to **La Trinité** by St-Waninge. A relic containing a phial of the Precious Blood of Christ is kept in an early 16th century marble tabernacle situated behind the alter. It was created in 1507 by the Italian sculptor Viscardo.

According to legend, Christians and in particular Isaac of Arimathea, hid the phial of blood in a fig tree and sent it to sea. It was later found washed ashore at Fécamp. **La Trinité** was briefly used as a burial church for various dukes and in fact its fourth chapel is the resting place for Abbot Volpiano. The baptismal chapel houses both the Normandy dukes

of Richard I and II.
The abbey also had its own angelic visitation before the Bishops in 943. A footprint to the right of the alter, marks this.
Open daily admission charge.
Tel: 00 33 32 35 28 84 39.

Opposite the Eglise de la Trinité are the ruins of the 11th century **Palais Ducal** - Duchy of Normandy. History has it that The Duke-King II Plantaget made the area into an impressive military fortress in the 12th century simply because he wanted to make the King of France jealous. As fate would have it the duchy was annexed to the Kingdom of France in 1204 anyway.

Palais Benedictine 110 rue Alexandre Le-Grand
The magnificent Palais Benedictine

is a building straight out of a fairy tale. It was built and completed in 1900, by Alexandre le Grand, a wines and spirit merchant. He was aware of an elixir created in the 16th century by a monk called Vincelli . Vincelli discovered the herbs, which now give the liqueur its flavour, growing freely on the local chalky cliffs. Alexandre le Grand brought the benedictine monk's concoction back to life and named it Bénédictine in memory of the monks. He added his motto of the order to the label abbreviated as D.O.M. which means Deo

Optimo Maximo - to God, the best and greatest. The Palais is both an art museum and a distillery. The museum has paintings, furniture, sculpture, ivory, plaster and wrought iron pieces housed in large rooms. The distillery produces the famous Benedictine liqueur. A tour around the distillery will not enlighten you to the exact nature of the secret recipe, but you can examine the 27 plants and spices from around the world, that are used in today's distillation method. The tour ends with a free tasting of liqueur Benedictine and an opportunity to buy a bottle on the way out. Guided tours last 1 1/2 hours.

Admission FF20.

Tel 00 33 32 35 10 26 10

NOTE: Buy a ticket for one of the following museums and entry to the other is free.

Musée Centres des Arts
21 rue Alexandre-Legros

Fécamp is also famous for Schuffenecker's painting at the Musée Centre des Arts. The charming palace is in a pedestrianized area in the centre of the old town. It has a collection of ivories and painted porcelain and statues rescued from decrepit churches. There's an assortment of miscellaneous items including a collection of baby's feeding bottles from antiquity to today.

Admission FF20.

Tel: 00 33 32 35 28 31 99

Musée des Terres-Neuvas et de la Pêche (Museum of the Newfoundland fishermen)
27 bd Albert 1

The museum aptly faces the sea for it reveals the history of the sea from the Viking invasions. It highlights the life of 19th century cod fishermen on the banks of Newfoundland featuring a large collection of marine paintings. Two floors contain miniature boats. The upper floor contains a scale model of the port and town as it was in 1830 in the pre-railway days. Exhibits also depict the art of smoking fish over the 'boucanes'. Captions are in French but English translations are available Closed Tuesday, open daily peak season. Admission FF20. Tel: 00 33 32 35 28 31 99

The D211 passes the small, peaceful and pleasant resort of **Yport,** a few miles west of Fécamp. The area has an impressive red-brick and limestone church, but it is almost hidden within a narrow gap in the chalky cliffs. Yport's shingle beach is speckled with brightly coloured boats making it pretty as a picture postcard with houses covered in flint shingles. These attributes have long made the resort a favourite point of inspiration among painters. Unlike Fécamp and Etretat, the atmosphere is slow and the locals tend to be quite insular. According to local

> **Tourist Office**
> 113 rue Alexandre-Legros
> Fécamp
> Tel: 00 33 32 35 28 51 01
>
> When it is very busy, there is a secondary tourist office opposite the holiday port.

legend, the area was colonized two thousand years ago by Greek fisherman from Asia Minor. The inhabitants today are their descendants. Amazingly though, everything seems to be open on a Sunday.

Beyond Yport, the winding roads lead to secluded valley of **Vaucottes** and the resort of **Vattetot-sur-Mer**. Turn right on to the D11 to descend to **Etretat**.

> At Etretat take a walk along the cliffs and see if you can find the elephant plunging its trunk into the waves.

So beautiful is the cliff face at Etretat that it became the inspiration for the impressionist art movement.

Etretat is the most beautiful and intriguing of the Alabaster coast's Norman seaside resorts. It is blessed with natural monumental arches within its cliff face featuring Victor Hugo's discovery of '*the biggest architecture that there ever was*'. He was describing an awsome 70 meter high needle behind which the manneporte is 90m high. So impressive are these visions that they were the inspiration for the impressionist art movement at the end of the 19th century. Artists such as Claude Monet, Eugène Delacroix and Gustave Courbet were quite simply moved to put paint brush to canvass. Even writers felt the need to put pen to paper to express their sentiments. Alphonse Karr, a writer of the 19th century, for example, wrote:

'If I had to show a friend the sea for the first time, I would do so at Etretat'

These visual treats can be experienced at the Falaise d'Amont (upstream cliff) where the view takes in the Falaise d'Aval (downstream cliff) and beyond. Its course runs above the steep shingle beach over-shadowed by the cliffs of Aval and Amont on either end. It is worth taking this

Oyster & The Queen

In 1777 Queen Marie-Antoinette holidayed in Etretat. After tasting the indigenous oysters, she became so addicted that she was compelled to have oyster parks built on the side of the cliffs, ensuring an abundant supply for herself.

invigorating - even if it is a little rugged - path westwards through Falaise d'Aval and pass the Manneport Arch. Taking the steps that connect with Falaise d'Amont you will pass the large 11th/12th century parish church **Notre Dame d'Etretat**. The treck to get up here is worth it just for the view of the so often painted arch of the Falaise d'Aval.

Back on low ground, there is a monument which is half bird, half concord, commemorating the pilots Nungessor and Coli. On 8th May 1927 these two French pilots attempted to fly across the Atlantic on board the White Bird and were never seen again. To find out more about this daring duo, visit the **Nungessor and Coli museum, Falais amont** which is dedicated entirely to them. Open: spring weekends , summer daily 10-12am & 2-6pm.

> ### The 'Man Hole' Legend
>
> Legend has it that in 1792 a Swedish ship was caught in a raging storm. It broke apart after bashing violently against the rocks. All but one of the crew died. Though he surrendered to the storm and passed out, a wave lifted and placed him onto a rocky ledge and away from death's door. Since then the cave has been known as the 'Man Hole'.

Moving away from the lure of the sea, the centre of Etretat also has its allure. In **place du Maréchal Foch**, there are some notable 16th century timber houses such as Le Tricorne and the Market Hall which hosts a covered market An unusual carving of a bat with a man's head overlooks the entrance of the market.

Other sights to see are:

Aquarium Marin
rue Jules Gerbeau

The aquarium is built into the cliffs in a tunnel at 'le parc de loisirs des Roches'. It houses marine species from tropical seas and the Channel. Open weekends 2- 6pm Easter-September.
Tel: 00 33 32 35 27 01 23

Le Chateau Des Aygues
Rue Offenbach

The Queens of Spain once resided here. Furniture and souvenirs of the royal families of the 19th century are on display, including objects of Chinese extraction. Guided tours in English. Admission FF30. Open July-August from 2-6pm.
Tel 00 33 32 35 28 92 77

Le Clos Lupin
rue Guy de Maupassant

The family home of Maurice Leblanc has a strange charm. Here visitors can solve the engimatic adventures of the 'gentleman burglar'. Lunch typical of the region, is available too in 'L'assiette d'Arsène'.
Tel: 00 33 32 35 27 08 23

For a pleasant evening in Etretat, the casino is a good bet. A little flutter can be followed by dinner and dance in the small but adequate nightclub.

Take the D940 direct to Le Havre

Tourist Office
Place Maurice-Guillard
Etretat
Tel:00 33 (0)35 27 05 21

Tourist Train
A tour between Etretat and Les Loges can be taken on a little puffing train which quaintly shuttles tourists.
Tel: 00 33 32 35 27 05 21.

The Market Place
place du Maréchal Foch
The daily market is dominated by various craftsmen exhibiting and selling their products.

Pop over to Forges Les Eaux for sheer enjoyment.

In the morning, visit a museum, admire the half-timbered buildings or perhaps some traditional pottery. In the afternoon set off for a ramble on foot, by bike or horseback in the most beautiful countryside Normandy has to offer. In the evening choose from 13 restaurants to taste the culinary delights of the Bray country and then try your luck at the Grand Casino in splendid surroundings. At the end of the evening return to your accommodation set in a tranquil natural environment.

Tranquillity, natural surroundings, good food, sports, leisure activities and dreams of fortune are all at your disposition - the choice is yours.

For further information, advance booking and free brochure, contact:

Tourism Board
4 rue du Maréchal Leclerc
F. 76440 Forges-Les-Eaux
Tel: 00 33 (0)235 90 52 10
www.ville-Forges-les-Eaux.fr

7 Hotels
11 Gîtes
13 Restaurants
120 camp sites

110 km from Paris
200km from Brussels
300km from London

From Calais take A16/A28 exit at Forges-les-Eaux
From Dieppe take D915
From Le Havre take A29/A28/D919

Le Havre

***In contrast to the Alabaster Coast
Le Havre is a very much a mundane city.
Behind the concrete jungle though
there is still some touristic appeal***

Le Havre, is the French word for haven. Unfortunately, it did not prove to be much of a haven when during the air raids of World War II it was bombed flat.

This little fishing village was transformed into a port by Francois I in 1517 and he named it rather modestly 'Francois-ville'. When the English took possession of the port (for just ten months) the name was changed to 'Havre-de-Grâce', - Haven of Grace. From then on, Le Havre has been modified and reshaped many times. The port was redesigned by Girolamo Bellarmato in 1525 and then enlarged and fortified under Cardinal Richelieu and Louis XIV and then further improved under Louis IVI in the 18th century. In the middle of the 19th century Napoleon III also took it upon himself to add to the improvement of Le Havre. Unfortunately, 400 years of construction and development was completely destroyed in World War II. These days the only notable pre-war building is the Notre Dame Cathedral.

Le Havre had to be rebuilt and the Parisian architect, Auguste Perret was commissioned with the task of redesigning Le Havre. Perret decided to create a very modern look with an angular grid of roads, using reinforced concrete as material for the buildings. The result is a rather monotonous grid of spacious streets and large expanses of public area. His designs earned him the imaginative nickname 'the magician of reinforced concrete!' On an overcast day, the grey uniform buildings tend to throw a rather bleak shadow over the area. In favour of the bias towards function over beauty, is that everywhere in Le Havre is accessible. Nevertheless, a good sense of direction paramount to navigate the busy forked roads and the bewildering one-way system. One deviation from your route and you may find yourself miles out of your way!

Le Havre, with its own airport and established sea links to Britain, has acquired a very commercial, vibrant character. It ranks 5th largest port in Europe and is France's biggest ocean port and certainly its premier port for foreign trade. The overall face of its 198,000 inhabitants is a young, cosmopolitan one with no less than six in ten people being under 40 years of age.

A peaceful part of Le Havre is the **Ste Adresse** area which appears to be the residential area. One section is known as le Nice Havrais, where the word 'Nice' (the English version) is a good description of the terraced villas facing the sea. The beach in this area is highly popular with windsurfers and in fact is ranked number 3 in France for this activity.

In even more contrast to the industrial facade, right in the heart of the city of Le Havre is the fabulous, serene 625-acre **forest of Montgeon** taking you away from the madding crowds. The 380-acre city park, **Rouelles** park, was created on the site of a former farm where the manor and dovecot have been preserved. As well as a perennial plant garden showing nature at its best there is an equestrian centre.

Le Havre

Tourist Office
186 boulevard Clémenceau
76600 Le Havre
Tel: 00 33 (0)232 74 04 04
Open: 9am-6.30pm
Monday to Saturday
10am-1pm Sunday

L'Hôtel de Ville -

The Town Hall, is huge. It has a 72m high concrete tower which can be seen from some distance.

Markets

Les Halles indoor market
Avenue René Coty
Open: Monday & Wednesday mornings and all day Friday.

Cours de la République
Open Tuesday, Thursday and Saturday all day.

Main Shopping Streets
- place de l'Hôtel de Ville
- rue de Paris
- place des Halles
- Quartier du Rond-Point
- rue Aristide Briand
- rue Maréchal Joffre
- course de la République.

To the west are Le Havre's 2km beach and pleasant promenade. The stretch of beach running parallel to **Boulevard Albert I** tends to be very lively. Its popularity apparently stems from its well equipped leisure complex. The locals and tourists alike enjoy the sports facilities, snack bars, restaurants and shops. The beach even comes complete with its own winding stream.

The oldest but livliest district - **Quartier St-François** - is flanked on either side by the two docks **Bassin du Roi** and the **Bassin du Commerce**. It is a self-contained island connected to the rest of Le Havre by bridges. It was once a fish market, but like the rest of Le Havre, it has also yielded to modernisation. The area is a full of nocturnal vibrancy and activity fuelled by a huge selection of restaurants and eateries. The area also plays host to the museum of old Le Havre.

The hub of Perret's new town is the **Place de l'Hôtel de Ville**. It is superbly situated on one of the largest squares in Europe forming part of Perrets rectangular grid. At the north end of the Square at **avenue Foch** is the **Hôtel de Ville,** the town hall, which serves to throw some decorative relief onto the square.

On a sunny day take a stroll through the leafy **avenue Foch.** The road leads to the fourteen storey buildings of the 'Porte Océane', to the beach and rue de Paris. and the ferry quays.

If it is raining, **rue de Paris**, is a good place to be since, with its grand concourse of shops, you can benefit from a good dose of retail therapy.

Top Shops for Women

Attitude
37 place des Halles Centrales
A good selection of Kenzo, Cerruti and Esprit fashion

Rive Gauche
64 rue bernardin-de-Saint-Pierre
This shops sells really good ready-to-wear clothes and accessories.

Viviana
1 rue Edouard-Herriot
Labels include Pierre Cardin, Christine Laure, Fred Sabatier. Sizes go up to size 52.

Top Shops for Men

Masculin Pluriel
37 rue du Président-Wilson
A range of Hugo Boss suits, Kenzo ties, and Sebago shoes.

Top Department Store

Les Nouvelles Galeries
37 rue de Paris

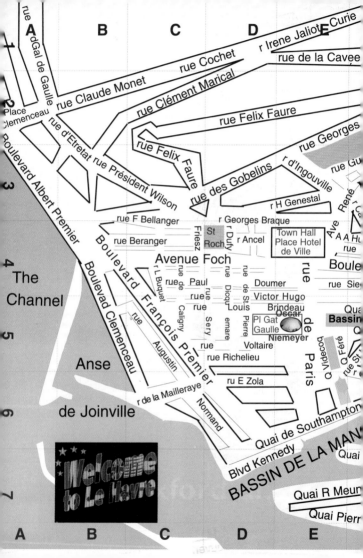

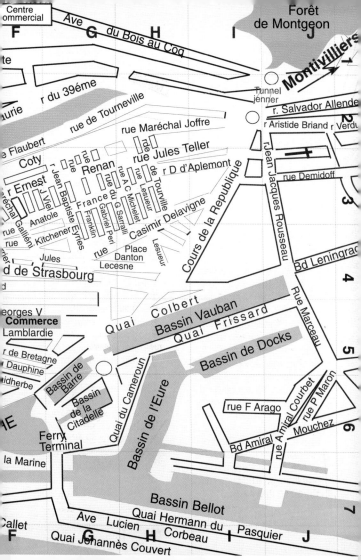

Musée de l'Ancien Havre
1 rue Jérôme Bellarmato

This museum - in a 17th century town house - has prints and watercolours of 'Vieux Havre' showing how Le Havre once looked. The history stems from 1517 covering the Renaissance and military periods and industrial revolution up to the end of the 19th century.

Closed Mon & Tues
Tel: 00 33 235 42 27 90

Preuré de Graville
1 rue Elisée Reclus

This 11th century church was built on the tomb of Sainte Honorine patron saint of bargemen and was once a place of pilgrimage. It was opened as a museum in 1929 in the 15th century Hôtel du Portugais building, and contains historical documents of the abbey and a large collection of religious art and statues. There is a statue of the black virgin in the garden.

Tel: 00 33 235 47 14 01

Espace Maritime des
Docs Vauban
quai Frissard

Originally the bonded warehouses were full of coffee, cotton and tobacco. The Maritime Exhibition Centre now contains a century and a half of fishing and other maritime history.

Tel 00 33 2 35 24 51 00

Musée des Beaux-Arts
André Malraux
Blvd John Kennedy

Prepare to be dazzled by this luminous building. Built in 1953-61 by Raymond Audigier and Guy Lagneau, the glass building is cleverly flooded by natural light regulated by a system of shutters and louvres. It houses collections of European paintings from the 17th to 20th centuries including works of the locally-born painters Raoul Dufy, Eugène Boudin and Monet. You name it, it exhibits it.

Closed: Tues.
Tel: 00 33 235 42 33 97

Muséum d'Histoire Naturelle
place Vieux Marché

This used to be the Palace of Justice but now exhibits items of zoology, mineralogy, ornithology, palaeontology and the works of the naturalist 19th century painter Lesueur. The building is one of the few historical monuments that survived the war.

Tel: 00 33 2 35 41 37 28

Church of Saint Joseph
Boulevard François 1er

A modern church built in the Perret style. It has two interesting features: At the apex of the 109m high tower is an octoganol bell tower which can be seen from a distance. Secondly is the clever diffusion of light with the use of simple, coloured window panes all around the church. The effect is an interplay of light entering the church from the east and west which focus on the altar.

Boat Trips
La Salamdre
Tel: 00 33 235 42 01 31

Yachting Port de Plaisance
boulevard Clémenceau
Tel: 00 33 235 22 72 72

Taxi-Tours
The driver speaks English
Tel: 00 33 232 74 74 00
(deposit 200FF)

Golf
Golf du Havre
route de St Suplix
76290 Octeville sur Mer
Tel: 0033 235 47 12 06

Musée Maison de L'Armateur
3 Quai de L'ille

Do you have an eye for decor? The building is a symbol of Le Havre's trade and prosperity and is testament to 18th century architecture.
Tel: 00 33 32 35 42 33 92

Notre-Dame Cathedral
Rue de Paris

A superb cathedral with a Gothic tower. It was badly damaged in 1944 but has been restored and has a preservation order on it.

Cultural Centre
Espace Oscar Niemeyer
nickname: The Volcano
or Yogurt Pot
Bassin du Commerce

The cultural centre was designed by the Brazilian architect Oscar Niemeyer and completed in1982. It is an immense piece of modern architecture with a slightly asymmetrical smooth radiant white cone resembling a ship's funnel with the overall shape resembling a volcano. The entrance is concealed by a white walkway into the plaza beneath. The interior of the volcano is made up of a theatre and two cinemas, restaurants and an outdoor exhibition room. A cupped copper hand fountain protrudes from the volcano inscribed as follows: *'one day, like this water, the land, beaches and mountains will belong to all'.*

Le Pont du Normandy
Normandy Suspension
Bridge

The Normandy bridge which crosses from Le Havre over the Siene river to give access to Lower Normandy is one of the longest suspension bridges in the world. It is a very elegant bridge by day and by night almost magical. The lights that illuminate the bridge at night giving its lovely glow were designed by the Brittany artist Yann Kersalé.

There is a price to pay to get across and this is in the region of FF30.

Normandy Bridge

Shopping in Le Havre

Auchan Hypermarket
Centre Commercial
Montiviliers La Lezarde

English: No
Tasting: No
Payment: £, Major currencies

Parking: Yes
Open: 10am to 8pm daily
Closed: Sunday

How To Get There

Exit customs at the ferry port. At the roundabout take 2nd exit. At the traffic lights turn right, - ignoring sign to Auchan telling you to turn left. Stay on the right hand lane and straight over the lights.Follow signs to Montivilliers, then Montivilliers La Lezarde and then finally signs to Centre Commercial taking an exit on the left.

There seems to be so many signs promoting Auchan hypermarket all over Le Havre, seemingly giving contradictory directions. It is all frustratingly confusing until you realise that there are in fact two Auchans being promoted via the billboards.

This particular branch of Auchan is situated in a massive shopping estate just on the periphery of Le Havre in an area called Montivilliers.

The Auchan complex itself, though dominated by Auchan Hypermarket, contains a myriad of other shops and service outlets.

Throughout the estate there are also hypermarket versions of Toys R Us, the Decathlon sports shop, a horticultural nursery and clothes and shoe supermarkets amongst others. The outlets are so big that just walking from one end of the estate to the other is a trek in itself.

Cave Danton
74 rue Casimir Delavigne
76600 Le Havre
Tel: 00 33 (0)235 41 27 37

English:	No
Tasting:	No
Payment:	FF
Parking:	A little difficult but on the road outside.
Open:	Tues-Sat 9.30am-12 noon & 2-5pm Sun 9am-12 noon
Closed:	Monday

How To Get There
From the port follow signs to Centre Ville over rue de 129iem, left into Boulevard Strasbourg, right into Jean Baptist Eyries, send right into rue Casimir Delavigne. The outlet is about 100 yards on the right

An attraction of this small outlet is that it has selection of 20 10 litre bag-in-the-box French wines which when opened, last 3 months. If you are buying in bulk this could be handy way of carrying your wines home. Another bonus is that it is open on Sunday mornings.

What's on offer at Cave Danton. - A selection.

Prices are in French Francs converted to Sterling at an exchange rate of FF10 to £1. All the following are quantities of 10 litres bag-in-the-box.

Red wines	FF	£
Vin de la Vallée du Rhône	110.00	11.00
St Chinian	120.00	12.00
Région de Bordeaux	130.00	13.00
Rosé wines		
Vin de la Vallée du Rhône	110.00	11.00
St Chinian	135.00	13.50
Région de Bordeaux	160.00	160.00
White Wines		
Vin Blanc Région Bordeaux	150.00	15.00
Muscadet Sur Lie Propriétaire Récoltant	195.00	19.50

Le Caves de la Transat

Avenue Lucien Corbeaux
76600 Le Havre
Tel: 00 33(0)235 53 66 65

English:	No
Tasting:	No
Payment:	FF
Parking:	Yes
Open:	Mon-Thurs 9.30am-12.30pm &1.30-6.30pm Sat 9.30am-12.30pm & 2pm to 6.30pm
Closed:	Fri, Sun, Mon

How To Get There

Exit customs at the port, at the roundabout take 3rd exit. At the end of the road turn left to roundabout. Take 3rd exit. Follow the road to the left the outlet is on the right.

L e Caves de la Transat seems isolated in an unkempt docklands area. Its own billboard is the only outward indication of any retail activity. However, after parking your car conveniently close to the entrance, and walking through the doors of the outlet, you will be met with an orderly layout of wines displayed on their boxes. A closer look reveals a quality range of French wines and Champagnes available in cases of 3, 6 and 12 bottles.

This outlet was once part of the famous Compagnie Générale Transatlantique known simply as Transat who, for 120 years ran a fleet of liners. When the last made her final voyage in 1974, a warehouse was opened in Le Havre to sell off the stock. Transat had always symbolised high quality to the public who rushed to buy what they could. To satisfy this demand a trading company was set-up.

The stock is still high quality but the service is not rushed so you may as well take your time choosing the wines that tickle your palate.

La Generale Des Vins

92 rue Dicquemare
76600 Le Havre
Tel: 00 33 (0)235 22 90 90
www.lageneraledesvins.fr

English: Yes
Tasting: ?
Payment: £, Major currencies

Parking: Yes
Open: 9am-12pm & 2pm-7pm daily
Closed: Sunday, Monday am

How To Get There

Exit customs at the port. At the roundabout take 3rd exit. At the end turn left sign posted Centre Ville. At roundabout take 1st exit sign posted Quartier St Francois. Cross the bridge, turn left into Quai Notre Dame, then right into Quai de Southampton and right into rue de Paris. Pass the volcano, turn left then 2nd right into rue Dicquemare.

Special Offer

5% off

wines & Champagnes
just show your guide to be eligible

Lots of quality vintage French wine on offer here mainly from Bordeaux, Burgundy, Rhône and the Loire. Professional advice is on offer too, though the English may be a little shaky, the ambience is friendly, so feel free to ask.

There are also a variety of whiskys and spirits alongside wine accessories for sale such as cork screws, glasses. thermometers and wine glasses.

Nicolas
Les Halles Centrales
rue Bernadin de St Pierre
76600 Le Havre
Tel: 00 33 (0)235 42 24 63

English: No
Tasting: No
Payment:

Parking: Yes
Open: Mon 2.30-7.30pm
Tues-Fri
8.30am-7.30pm
Closed: Sun

How To Get There
Exit customs at the port. At the roundabout take 3rd exit. At the end turn left sign posted Centre Ville. At roundabout take 1st exit sign posted Quartier St Francois. Cross the bridge and turn left into Quai Notre Dame, then right into Quai de Southampton and right into rue de Paris. Pass the volcano, turn left, left again and park in the car park. Nicolas is inside Halles Centrales indoor market.

Nicolas is one of France's oldest retail wine chains, perhaps the French answer to Victoria Wine. Certainly you are likely to find one in every town. This branch is situated within an indoor market and is surrounded by shops selling all manner of mouth watering products.

The range of wine at this quaint outlet is almost all medium priced French wines starting from as low as FF11 and Champagnes from around FF130.

The range also includes the odd bottle from Spain and Chile.

Les Vignerons Reunis

71-73 rue Jean-Jacques
Rousseau
76600 Le Havre
Tel: 00 33 (0)235 42 64 36

English:	A little
Tasting:	En vrac wines
Payment:	£, 💳 💳
Parking:	On the road outside
Open:	Daily 8am-12pm & 2pm-7pm
Closed:	Sun-Mon

A spacious yet quaint outlet decorated Normandy style with timber girders. All around are variously packaged red, white and rosé wines, either 'en vrac' (huge cylinders contain wine which is cyphoned off to order), bag-in-the-box, in bottles or in wood barrels.

Wines en vrac are generally country or table wines and bought this way tend to be very good value. For example, a popular country wine such as Vin de Pays de l'Herault

How To Get There
Exit the port, at roundabout take 1st exit into Quai Frissard, at the crossroads turn left into Jean-Jacques Rousseau.

is offered en vrac at just FF8.40 a litre and Muscadet is offered en vrac at FF18.30 a litre. Feel free to try before you buy any of the en vrac wines to ensure the wine is palatable.

Special Offer

10% off

Bag-in-the-box and wines en vrac

show your guide to be eligible

Les Vins de la Gironde

43 rue Sadi Carnot
76620 Le Havre
Tel: 00 33 (0)235 46 01 66

English:	A little.
Tasting:	En Vrac only
Payment:	💳 💳
Parking:	On the street
Open:	8.30am-12.30pm & 4-7pm
Closed:	Sunday & Monday am

How To Get There

Exit the port, at roundabout take 3rd exit and turn left at the junction. At roundabout take 2nd exit, cross bridge onto Quai Southampton. At roundabout take 1st exit, turn right into Bvd Francois 1st. At roundabout take 1st exit onto rue Gullemard. At lights cross into Clement Marical. Turn right sign posted Parc de Montgeon into rue de la Cavée Verte After sports ground turn left.

I f you wish to experience a glimpse of French life and come away with some fine wine as well, then a detour to this old-fashioned 'cave' is strongly recommended.

Le Vins de la Gironde is situated in Le Havre's oldest cellar probably dating back to the creation of Le Havre itself. It seems not much has changed here with the passage of time. The weathered front door opens into a small shop, rife with a pungent vinous aroma in the air.

Though set in a quiet back street, the shop is busy with a constant trickle of locals meandering in and out to buy their cidre or wine. They chat and joke amiably amongst themselves and with Mr Duboc the proprietor while he cheerfully serves them. They are, it seems,

Special Offer

FREE
bottle of wine
each time you visit
this outlet !
Just show your guide

happy to wait however long it takes to get served.

Hanging listlessly from a small hole in the wall by the front door is a hose. It doesn't stay listless long before being used to cyphone off cider from a hidden container into recycled bottles.

The shelves in the shop are stacked with empty wine bottles, for reasons unknown; perhaps Mr Duboc keeps them there as representation of the stock in the cellar.

A small stairway leads into the basement cellar which stretches back a fair way. This authentic musty cellar contains a large stock of wines and huge wood barrels from

which wine is sold en-vrac. You can try before you buy any of en-vrac wines so feel free to ask. Mr Duboc recommends the following red wines and has reduced their price to tempt you to buy them. These are:

Morgon
Dmn de Lathevalle 1998
FF48.40

Le Vigneau
St Nicolas-de-Bourgogne
FF27.80

Château La Courtiade
Peyvergès 1998
FF28.60

Cheers!

The Wine & Beer Company

Quai Frissard
Bassin Vauban
76600 Le Havre
Tel: 00 33 (0)235 26 38 10
www.wineandbeer.co.uk

English: Yes
Tasting: A Little
Payment: £, Major currencies

Parking: Yes
Open: 10am-10pm Mon-Sat
10am-4pm Sun

How To Get There
At the first roundabout after leaving customs take the first exit, cross the bridge. The Wine & Beer Company warehouse is on the right.

Apart from being the closest wine outlet to the port, The Wine and Beer Company is the only outlet in Le Havre that sells a range of international wines alongside their French selection. Pop into their warehouse when you leave customs and you will be able to purchase reasonable wines for less than £1.00! Try the Hock which is fruity enough for just 89p for a whole litre! The fizz looks good too. Try the uncomplicated, easy-to-drink Great Western Brut Rosé at £3.19. The Champagne selection comes with appealing price tags. For example Pol Roger at £13.79 and a house Champagne at just £8.99 - can't be bad!

The beer range includes Lowenbrau 50cl cans for £9.99 for 24 amongst other popular brands.

Special Offer

Spend £25.00 on table wine and get a free case of Wendelbrau 24 x 25cl 5.2% ABV
on production of your guide

**Rouen , the capital of Upper Normandy
is oozing with touristic appeal, but not just on ground
level. Raise your eyes to enjoy a skyline dominated
by spires and church towers**

The lovely town of Rouen is just one hour's drive from both the ports of Le Havre and Dieppe, and just over one hour away from Paris. It stands within a valley astride the Seine and is surrounded by huge forests and wooded hills.

It is the oak from these woodlands that was used to build the attractive half-timbered houses that are peculiar to the area.

There are over 700 of these remarkable houses, generally painted in subdued reds, pinks and browns. They are so pretty that they quaintly adorn the cobbled and sometimes twisting streets of the old city of Rouen.

The medieval centre of old Rouen, on the north bank of the Seine, seems almost ergonomically designed, being easy to find and everything worth visiting seems to hand. In In effect, the pulse of the town beats within a defined walkable area. By stark contrast new Rouen on the other side of the Seine has an official feel containing mainly offices and tower blocks.

The early Celtic settlers who established a trading centre on the banks of the Seine were attracted by the forests and the ease of access to the river. The area soon became the capital of the Vilocasses but was taken over by the Romans and became known as Rotumagos. The Viking Rollo was baptised here in 911 and made Rouen his capital. He cleaned up the river and built a series of quays and Rouen soon became a prosperous and charming city.

From 970 onwards the **Place du Vieux Marché - the old market square,** was imaginatively restored, redeveloped and relaid in a triangular shape and was once the market square of medieval Rouen.

In 1204 Normandy was annexed to France but the traditional trading links with England continued.

In 1419 the English captured Rouen and this led to the most notable event in Rouen's history - the burning at the stake of Joan of Arc on May 30th, 1431 for alleged witchcraft. The sombre site at the **Place du Vieux Marché** is well marked with a mosaic stone and a huge 29m high cross called **la Croix de la Réhabilitation.** It has an almost haunting presence. Eventually in 1449, Rouen was returned to French hands.

Joan of Arc was canonised in 1920 and afterwards became the country's patron saint. By 1964 regional authorities were in place, and since then Rouen has been the capital of Upper Normandy.

In 1969 Louis Arretche was commissioned to design a memorial church, which was completed in 1979. This is an ultra modern, wacky church which stands alongside the memorial site. Its circular interior shape means that congregants sit in a semi circle before the pulpit and as with traditional churches, it has superb stained glass windows. Its very elongated roof serves as the roof of a

walkway and a small,

trendy fish and vegetable market. Opposite, the old buildings across the square house a selection of restaurants which overlook the church.

Over the last 50 years, much of the architecture in Rouen had to be rebuilt after the destruction of the second world war. The architect, Louis Arretche supervised the project and enormous sums were spent. The right bank was restored to the urban layout that existed prior to the war, but the left bank, suffered total eradication. It had to be completely redesigned producing a modern urban district.

Rouen is well-known for

its fine and extensive collection of stained glass. In fact, most churches have their own range dating from different periods. The most extensive collection - which includes all periods dating back from 1200 - are represented in Rouen's **Cathédral Notre Dame** on **place de la Cathédral**. The famous painter Monet, who had

Notre Dame Cathedral

lodgings within a building close by - which today houses the tourist office - started the glass painting of the cathedral in the 11th century and this trend continued over the next eight centuries.

Gastronomy, as everywhere in France, is highly respected in Rouen as is typical of the French, and Rouen is certainly not short of restaurants. Regional dishes include duck paté, Normandy sole, pressed Rouen duck, Rouen sheep's foot amongst others. So concerned are the people of Rouen in preserving their culinary traditions that in 1986 a society was formed calling itself l'Order des canardiers -  The Order of the Duck. Its sole purpose is the preservation of culinary art symbolised by the regional recipe of Rouen Duck. Try it and if you like it, let us know.

Bon appetite!

Tourist Office
It is housed in the early 16th century 'House of the Exchequer'.
25 place de la Cathédral
BP 666, 76008 Rouen
Open 9am - 6pm.
Closed 1.30-2.30pm
Tel: 00 33 32 32 08 32 40

Tourist Office Services
Hotel Reservation Service
Foreign Exchange.

Walks
There are many walking tours to choose from for different areas of the city which all start from the tourist office. Cost: FF35.

Petit Train
Starting at the tourist office there is a daily train which makes a 40 minute tour around Rouen. The train leaves hourly between 10am to 5pm. Cost FF35.

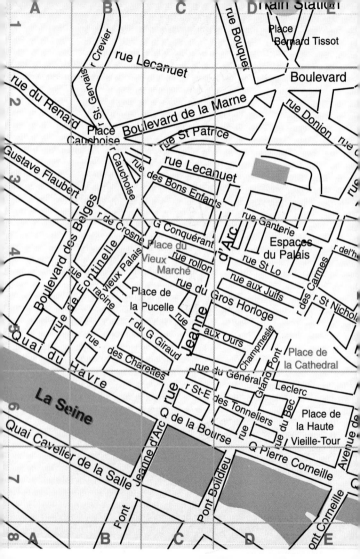

Rouen spends more of its budget on monuments than any other provincial French town. Monuments, Churches, Cathedrals, Gardens, Rouen has got it all

Joan of Arc Memorial place du Vieux-Marché

You cannot miss the 20m high cross and plaque commemorating Joan of Arc's burning at the stake.

Joan of Arc Church place du Vieux-Marché

The church sits alongside the Joan of Arc memorial site. Designed by Louis Arretche, The best description is that it is unusual, with bizarre spikiness. It is supposed to represent either an upturned boat or the flames at the stake. The roof tiles look much like fish scales and these match the fish-shaped windows of the church. The unusual roof is elongated to cover the walk way and a market across the square. Admission is free. Open Monday-Thursday & Saturday 10am-12.30pm & 2-6pm. Friday-Sunday 2-6pm. The covered market is open daily except Monday.

Musée départemental des Antiquités Square André Maurois, 198 rue Beauvoisine

The museum building is a 17th century monastery devoted to collections from pre-history to the 19th century. There are many archaelogical, Gallo-Roman collections such as the mosaic of Lillebonne and Merovingian periods. Art objects from the middle ages and Rennaissance furniture such as the 15th century tapestry of the 'Winged Deer' are also on display. Closed Tuesday. Open: 10am-12.30pm & 1.30-5.30pm. Admission FF20. Tel: 00 33 32 35 98 55 10

Musée de Joan of Arc
33 place du Vieux-Marché

On the south side of the square, behind a Joan of Arc souvenir gift shop, is a privately owned Joan of Arc museum. The shop looks tiny but as you walk through the doors to the museum, you will be amazed at how big it is. There are waxwork scenes depicting the events leading up to Joan of Arc's burning at the stake together with copies of manuscripts.

Open daily except Monday
10am to 6.30pm
Closed 12-2pm.

Joan of Arc had a heavenly visitation urging her to lead the French army

Tour Jeanne d'Arc
rue Bouvreuil
Junction rue du Donjon & rue du Cordier

This wafer thin tower is the remains of the castle of Philippe-Auguste (1205) and is where Joan of Arc was held in the torture chamber and tried. On that on day May 9 1431 Bishop Cauchon threatened her:

'There is the rack, and there are its ministers. You will reveal all now or be put to the torture.'

Her reply '
I will tell you nothing more than I have told you; no, not even if you tear the limbs from my body. And even if in my pain I did say something other-wise, I would always say afterwards that it was the torture that spoke, not I.'

At the site there is a model of the fortress and some pretty wells. She was actually held prisoner at the Tour de la Pucelle which was demolished in 1809.

Admission FF10.
Closed Tuesday Open 10am-noon & 2pm-5pm.

Cathédrale
de Notre Dame
Place de la Cathédrale

A short walk from the Gros Horloge on the site of a 3rd century AD Roman place of worship is this fabulous cathedral. This Gothic masterpiece was built during the 11th, 12th and 13th centuries. Later the **Tour de Beurre** - Butter Tower - was added and completed in 1506 and endowed with 56 bells. This odd name was the result of an erroneous belief that wealthy churchgoers met the cost of its erection through dispensations to eat butter during the Lent fast. The iron spire of the central lantern tower was added later and at 150m is the tallest in France.

Inside, look at the crypt which came to light during Lanfrey's excavations in 1934 (guided tour only), the chapel of Virgin Mary and the the tombs of the Dukes of Normandy (including Rollo's). Of course do not miss the stained glass windows - the result of nine centuries of work.

Open daily 8am-6pm

Musée de la Ferronnerie
Le Secq des Tournelles
2 rue Jacques Villon

Built in 16th century the church of Saint-Laurent houses the biggest collection in the world of over 5,000 items of ironwork from antiquity to the 20th century. Closed Tuesday. Open 10-1pm & 2-6pm Admission FF15 Tel:00 33 32 35 52 00 62.

Musée de la Céramique
1 rue Faucon

The museum is a 17th century palace with a collection of earthenware of Rouen. Other faience and porcelain centres in France and around the world are also included.

Closed Tuesday. Open: 10am-1pm & 2-6pm.
Admission FF15.
Tel: 00 33 32 35 88 42 92

Musée national de
l'éducation
185 rue Eau de Robec

Would you like to see what a 1900's classroom looked like? A visit here will tell all along with the history of education from 16th century.

Open 9am-12 & 1-5pm
Tel: 00 33 32 32 82 95 95

Musée Corneille
4 rue de la Pie

This is where Pierre Corneille was born in 1606. The museum contains a reconstruction of his study where he wrote Le Cid and Horace. The period furniture on show was not actually his. The library contains beautiful original editions of his work.
Closed Tuesday. Open: 10am-12.pm & 2pm-6pm. Admission FF5.
Tel: 00 33 32 35 71 63 92

Musée Flaubert et
d'histoire de la Médecine
51 rue de Lecat

This 18th century building is the birthplace of writer Gustave Flaubert and you can see the room of his birth. His father Achille-Cléophas Flaubert was a surgeon at the Hôtel-Dieu. Exhibits include advances in medicine in his time including anatomical curiosities, infirmary, pharmaceutical bowls and surgical instruments. There are also statues of healing saints. Closed Sunday and Monday. Open 10am-12pm & 2-6pm Admission FF12.
Tel 00 33 32 35 88 02 70

Gros Horloge et Beffroi
rue du Gros Horloge

Gros Horloge is a colourful, ornate clock with just one hand and a golden face resembling the flames of the sun. The clock dates back to the 14th century, and is one of the oldest functioning clocks in Europe. Its unique face shows the phases of the moon, and if you twist your neck a little you can glimpse the scene of the shepherd with his sheep. The clock sits on a Rennaissance style stone archway spanning the width of rue du Gros-Horloge. The road runs between two squares, Place de la Cathédrale and Place du Vieux-Marché and is probably the busiest street in the city. You can climb the bellfry's many steps to see its workings and at the top, enjoy the view of the old city. Every day at 9pm the bell still rings out the Conqueror's Curfew.

Musée Fluvial et Portuaire
bd Emile Duchemin, hangar portuaire 13

This riverside hangar was built in 1926 and belongs to the Shiaffins company. Rouen's maritime heritage can be discovered here. There are 30 boats on display including the barge 'Red Pompom'.
Open May-Nov, Mon-Fri 10am-12pm & 2-5pm, Sat/Sun 2-5pm.
Admission FF15
Tel: 00 33 32 10 15 51

Musée des Beaux Arts
Square Verdrei, 26 bis, rue Jean-Lecanuet

Inside this museum is an incredibly rare collection of 3000 paintings, 400 sculptures and 7000 drawings presented in chronological order dating from the Renaissance period. Artists include Clouet, Poussin, Caravaggio, Velasquez, Monet and Sisley.
Closed Tuesday.
Open: 10am-6pm.
Admission FF20.
Tel: 00 33 32 35 71 28 40.

Palais de Justice
rue aux Juifs

This superb Gothic style building was chosen to house the debating chamber and law court in 1515 when Normandy was granted its own parliament. The main building was built in 1509 and its two wings are date from 15th and 18th century.

When the courtyard was excavated in 1976, remains of an 11th century Romanesque building were found. Graffiti and Hebrew inscriptions on the walls suggest that the remains were of a synagogue, or perhaps a Jewish school. It is now referred to as Monument Juif, Jewish monument and is the oldest Jewish building in France.
Open Wed 2-6pm. Thurs-Mon 10am-6pm.

Abbataile Saint Ouen
Nr the Town Hall

This is one of the most stunning examples of the High Gothic style of architecture. Built during the 14th-16th centuries it is distinguishable by its elongated shape.

Jardin des Plantes de Rouen
Avenue des Martyrs de la Résistance

A beautiful 10 hectare garden, situated in the heart of Rouen. It belongs to the city and comprises both the botanical and the landscape with a huge variety of visual treats such as a 19th century orangery, a rose garden, hothouses and an 1842 pavilion. Included in the floor show is a collection of a rockery, medicinal plants, and rare trees.
Open daily 8am to dusk.
Tel 00 33 32 18 21 30

Expotec 103
13 rue St-Gilles

The windmill of Saint-Gilles exhibits the history of early techniques, tools machines, steam engines, a forge and looms.

Active Leisure

Golf de Rouen
18 holes, rue Francis Poulens 76130 Mont-Saint-Aignan
Tel: 00 33 32 35 76 38 65

Road Train
Visit the historical heart of the city by train.
Tel: 00 33 32 32 10 24 70

River Boating
Pick it up at the Port de Plaisance
Tel: 00 33 32 35 07 33 94

Sailing
ASPTT Rouen
27 rue Jean-Philippe Rameau 7600 Rouen
Tel: 00 33 32 35 12 65 40

Yacht Club Rouen 76, 1444 chausée Bertrand, 76840 Hénouville
Tel: 00 33 32 35 32 06 41

Mer amitié, 75 rue Jeanne d'Arc 76000 Rouen
Tel: 00 33 32 35 98 23 95

Seine Cruises
Le Cavelier de la Salle - a visit of the port of Rouen 25 place de la Cathédrale BP666, 76008 Rouen Cedex
Tel: 00 33 32 32 08 32 40

Shopping Districts

Just around the corner from the cathedral is **Rue Saint-Nicolas,** a pretty road laced with ancient courtyards - shopaholics will love it. This delightful road is great for clothes, featuring companies like **Lacoste**, as well as toys, antiques, and jewellry. If you like kitch, e.g. orange stools, black vinyl and mauve plastic then be sure to visit **Les Shadoks** at number 17.

There's more shopping choice, chain-store style on **rue du Gros Horloge** - the best known road in Rouen. Shops such as **Naf-Naf C&A**, **Levi's**, **Etam**, **Esprit**, **Morgan**, **Darjeeling** (for lovely lingerie) **Yves Rocher** (for perfume and beauty products) and the French supermarket **Monoprix** grace the road.

Rue du Gros Horloge is also home to a myriad of shoe shops. If you like Kickers footwear then try **France Arno** at number 44. If you prefer to take

Top Shops for Antiques
Chasset
rue de la Crox de Fer
An interesting antique shop with a range which includes toys and furniture.

Top Shops for Kids
Catimini
rue des Carmes
Classy clothing for kids.

La Fontaine Marmitaine
rue du Gros Horloge
A toy shop in a typically timbered building full of rocking horses, puppets, teddies, soldiers etc.

Department Stores
C& A
143 rue du Gros Horloge
True to the familiar style

Nouvelles Galeries
25 rue Grand Pont
Huge fashion collection

Printemps
4 rue du Gros Horloge
The Debenhams of Rouen

In The Best Possible Taste
La Caterie
159 rue du Gros Horloge
Good for saucy presents

your next step with Ted Lapidus then visit **Pallio** at number 15. Also on this road is a shoe shop called **Jonak**. Their promotions seem incredible. From time to time they even have a 'buy one pair, get one pair free' promotion which to bargain hunters has to be irresistible.

A few minutes away is **rue des Carmes.** This road is another good place to come shopping. Here you will find **Marks and Spencer, Cacharel**, a stylish fashion store, and nearby, a wonderful specialist perfume shop called **Sephora**.

Turn the corner into **rue Ganterie** to shop for young fashion at **Benetton** at number 25 and **Newman** at number 37. The well-known shoe shop **Bally** is at number 29 - still reassuringly expensive. If Doctor Martin footwear is more your style then **Halles Version Globo Loco** at number 98 has an impressive collection of these elegant shoe forms.

Top Shops for Women

Cacharel
111 rue des Carmes
Tailored, classy clothing for the woman who wants to be noticed, not loud.

Passion
80 rue Saint-Romain
If you love labels, this is for you. Names include Kenzo, Chantal, Thomass, Etienne and Opox Rapax.

Hermes
5 rue de Change
A famous brand known for its classic square print.

Top Shops for Men

Une Classe a Part
2 rue Croix de Fer
Designer clothes from Hugo Boss and Kenzo

Giovanni Pivetta
57 rue du Général-Leclerc
Suits to do business in. Hugo Boss, Cerruti are included in the selection.

Les Pionniers Marlboro Classics
39 rue de l'Hôpital
Jeans, rain and leather coats/jackets shirts, shoes and leather bags

Which Wine?

France is one of the leading wine producing countries in the world and this is reflected in the French outlets where most, if not all, of their selection is French. With so much choice, it helps to know a little about French wine.

Firstly, inspect the label for an indication and therefore an assurance of the quality of the wine. The best wines of the regions have Appéllation Contrôlées on the label which gives a guarantee of the origin, supervision of production method, variety of grape and quantity produced.

Less controlled but still good value wines, are listed as Vins Délimités de Qualité Supérieure (VDQS) and are worth trying. There are also the Vins de Pays. These are country wines, more widely found in the South of France, which do not specify the exact location of the vineyard but are generally worth a try and often offer the best value for money. Good examples are Vin de Pays du Gard and the wines from Côtes de Gascogne. Further down the ladder are the Vins de Table. They are varied in quality but are so cheap that they are worth a gamble. You could be surprised for as little at FF5-12.00 (50p-£1.20).

We have very broadly categorised the wine growing areas into seven major regions.
These are: Alsace, Burgundy, Bordeaux, Champagne, Loire, Midi and Rhône.

Alsace

The Alsace is situated in Eastern France on the German border. The wine labels from this area differ from the rest of France by calling the wine by the name of the grape rather than the area e.g. Gewürztraminer, Riesling.

If a label reads Alsace AC, this is the standard Alsace wine which is typically Germanic in character, often being aromatic and fruity, but drier than its German equivalent.

A label with Alsace Grand Cru printed on it indicates a higher quality and only the four most highly regarded grape types can be used in its making and they are: Gewürztraminer, Riesling (not to be confused with the German wine of the same name), Tokay Pinot and Muscat. These are medium priced white wines with reliable quality and are generally dry to medium dry. The Alsation wines are great aperitifs and also combine well with fish, poultry, salads or with a summer meal.

Expect to pay: 15-30 francs (£1.50-£3.00) per bottle.

Bordeaux

Bordeaux is in the South West region of France with the Dordogne region on its eastern border and the Atlantic ocean on the west.

The term Claret refers to the red dry wines of this region including those from the Médoc, St. Emillion and Pomerol which are reasonable wines in the lower price range.

There are also numerous wines known by the name of the Château. Quality, especially at the lower end, can be variable so spending a little more is a good taste investment. Claret goes well with meat, chicken and cheese.

Expect to pay: From as little as 14 francs (£1.40) per bottle, to more than 100 francs (£10.00) for a top class Château.

Which Wine?

Situated between Bordeaux and the Dordogne valley is an area called Bergerac.

Bergerac has a complete range of wines all of its own. The most commonly found are the simple red, rosé and dry white Bergeracs. Labels with Côtes de Bergerac are red and medium sweet white wines. Monbazillac produce inexpensive but good sweet dessert wines. Pércharmant is a fine red wine from this area.

Expect to pay: 10-16 francs (£1-£1.60) for Bergerac. 30 francs (£3) for Monbazillac.

Burgundy

Burgundy is situated south-east of Paris running from Chablis at the northern end, down through to Lyon at the southern end. About 75% of the wine production in this region is red with the remainder white. Almost all the white Burgundy wine is made with Chardonnay with a pinch of Pinot Blanc and Pinot Gris and the reds from the Pinot Noir grape. Bourgogne Passe-Tout Grains is a red Burgundian wine made from one-third Pinot Noir and two-thirds Gamay grapes

It is worth noting the area on the label when choosing a Burgundy wine since the more exact the area, the finer the wine is likely to be.

LE SOMMELIER *Jean-Marie Boudard extends a warm welcome, expert advice and wine-tasting at his wine shop. Discover new wines and choose from a huge range of quality wines, beers & spirits. You can find Le Sommelier near la Place Louise Vitet & Saint Jacques church.*

27 rue de Maillots, 76200, Dieppe
Tel: 02 35 06 05 20
Fax: 02 35 82 10 98
See page 29 for a special offer.

The best are labelled 'Grand Cru',followed by 'Premier Cru', 'Villages', a specified region and finally, the most basic will have just Burgundy.

The white Burgundian wines labelled Aligoté, are named after the grape they are made from. Expect a far sharper tang on the palate from the Aligoté than the Chardonnay grape can give. It is also an ideal wine to use to make a really good glass of Kir.

The best known of the whites, labelled Chablis, tend to be priced quite expensively. The problem with Chablis is its unreliability. When good, it is really good but the name itself is no guarantee.

The area of Côte d'Or can be divided into two wine producing regions, the Côte de Beaune and the Côtes de Nuits. Côte de Beaune produces some of the finest such as the lush Meursault. Some good light dry wines come from

Mâconnais such as Mâcon Blanc and Pouilly Fuissé. The white wines from the Mâconnais area are a much more palatable buy than their red counterparts, probably because white wine is more prevalent in the area.

The finest red Burgundy wine comes from the Côtes de Nuits such as Nuits St Georges and the Côtes de Beaune namely Pommard, Volnay and Monthélie. These are best drunk with meat, game and cheese.

All Burgundy white wines are dry and are an ideal accompaniment for fish.

Expect to pay: 35-70 francs (£3.50-£7.00) These wines tend to be reliable in this price bracket.

Probably the best known wine producing area in France is situated in the South of this region. It is the red wine producing area - Beaujolais, known mainly for its red-fruit scented wines, whose light hearted bubblegum flavours make them so easy to drink.

The Beaujolais wine is divided into the standard Beaujolais AC, Beaujolais Superieur which denotes a slightly higher alcohol content (not superiority) and Beaujolais-Villages which is an appéllation controlée (quality control), an award given to about 40 villages and considered to be of superior quality

The most prestigious of the Beaujolais wines bear the name of one of the ten communes (Crus). These are worth noting since you will come across them practically everywhere. These are Saint-Amour, Juliénas, Chénas, Moulin-à-Vent, Fleurie, Chiroubles, Morgon, Brouilly, Côte de Brouilly and Régnié (the most recently created, but least distinguished Cru).

These are medium priced red dry fruity wines with the Villages and Communes especially reliable and should be drunk young and served slightly chilled.

Expect to pay: 10-25 francs (£1-£2.50) for basic Beaujolais AC. 15-45 francs (£1.50-£4.50) per bottle for Beaujolais-Villages or named Commune.

Midi
(Languedoc Roussillon & Provence). The region stretches from north east of Marseilles down to the west of Perpignan bordering Spain. Wines from this region, such as Minervois and Corbières represent good value dry reds. The Vin de Pays (Country Wines) of the area offer the best value of all. The label will always show the Vin de Pays description followed by the region.

Expect to pay: 6-20 francs (60p-£2) per bottle and a little more if VDQS (Vins Délimités de Qualité Supérieure) is printed on the label.

Rhône
This area is located south of the Burgundy region and continues due south to the Mediterranean near Marseilles. The region generally produces robust,

Which Wine?

syrah grape based full bodied wines.

There is the standard Côtes du Rhône and the Côtes du Rhône Villages which is famous for its dry red wine. If the wine is attributable to a named village (which is shown on the label) the chances are it will be better quality but naturally more expensive. Côtes du Rhône wines accompany cheese and poultry dishes very well.

Southern Rhône harbours the Châteauneuf-du-Pape appellation. An amazing range of 13 grapes are permitted in the making of the wine of the same name, and sometimes truly fine wines are created here.

Expect to pay: 8-20 francs (80p-£2) for Côtes du Rhône label wines. 20-30 francs (£2-£3) for Côtes du Rhône Villages.

Loire
The Loire wine region starts at Nantes on the Western Atlantic coast of France and follows the Loire river east to Orléans where it cuts back south-east to Sancerre. The majority of wines produced in this area are white.

The Loire offers the widest variety of wine of any area in France and all have a certain refreshing quality that comes from the northerly position of most of the major Loire vineyards and the character of the soil.

Amongst the many well-known names from this area are Muscadet, Gros Plant Du Nantais, Poully-Fumé and Sancerre being examples of dry whites, and Anjou which is well known for its Rosé.

The versatile rosés can be drunk anytime with anything. The whites are best with fish and salads.

Although named wines are generally a better buy, in our experience it is especially true for Muscadet where we recommend either a named or 'sur lie' over the ordinary Muscadet.

Which Wine?

Expect to pay: 8-15 francs (80p-£1.50) for Gros Plant.
10-22 francs (£1-£2.20) for Muscadet.
35-39 francs (£3.50-£3.90) for Sancerre & Pouilly Fumé
10-16 francs (£1-£1.60) for Anjou Rosé wines.

If you prefer a medium dry wine then try the Vouvray at 20-25 francs (£2-£2.50). Vouvray is also available as a sparkling wine.

Champagne
'I am drinking stars'
Dom Perignon describing his sparkling wine

The most luxurious drink in the world, sparkling wine, suggests celebration - something special. Situated north east of Paris with Reims and Epernay at the heart of the area, Champagne is renowned for sparkling wine. The climate, the soil, the art of the wine maker and of course the grapes all combine to make Champagne the most celebrated in terms of unmatched quality and reputation. These are usually sold under a brand name e.g. Bollinger, Moët et Chandon, Mumm, Veuve Clicquot etc. which are nearly always dry. If you do not like dry wines, then ask for a demi-sec or even a rosé Champagne. Only wine made in the Champagne area is entitled to be called Champagne. Other wines of this type are referred to as 'sparkling' wine. Some have Méthode Traditionnelle on the label which means made in the Champagne method'.

Expect to pay: 60-70 francs (£6-£7) for lesser known brands.
120 francs (£12) upwards for well-known brands.

Champagne comes in the following sizes	
Quart:	20cl
Half-bottle:	37.5cl
Bottle:	75cl
Magnum:	2 bottles
Jeroboam:	4 bottles
Mathusalem:	8 bottles
Salmanazar:	12 bottles
Balthazar:	16 bottles
Nebuchadnezzar:	20 bottles

The Spirits of Normandy

***No vineyards here, but who cares,
in Normandy the apple
is triumphant!***

In Normandy, the apple has its place in all things grastronomique and that includes the various liquid nectars that are brought forth by fermented and distilled apple juice: Cider, Calvados and Pommeau.

Cider

A wide variety of apples are grown in Normandy, and a high proportion are fated to become cider. The different soils from the various apple growing areas endow their fruit with idiosyncrasies which can be tasted later in an extraordinary variety of ciders.

Good cider (bon bère) is made from apple juice. By law it has to be at least 5% alcohol. The process of secondary fermentation in the bottle results in a naturally sparkling drink (cidre bouché) and can cost between FF15-FF100. Like wine it can be medium, dry or sweet but may be very alcoholic and like Champagne it comes with a cork to pop.

Though most cider is factory made, an organisation, 10km South of Dieppe called Duche de Longueville, are reviving the old-fashioned brew using a single variety of apple. You can visit the brewery and taste the cider from June to September.

Where to Buy Cider

Cidrerie et Vergers du Duché de Longueville
Anneville-sur-scie
10km South of Dieppe
Tel: 00 33 (0)235 04 63 70

Cidrerie Pontreue
98 rue de Reims, Rouen
Tel: 00 33 (0)235 71 28 27

Most Normans suggest that cider is best served in pottery jugs and ideally should be drunk with shellfish, chicken, tripe or a lamb meal.

Calvados

Calvados, one of France's most sought after brandies, can be dated back to the 16th century, when Gilles de Gouberville, a French farmer, referred to it as 'eau-de-vie de cidre' in his diary. Three centuries later, apple brandies made in Normandy acquired the name of Calvados. Though the emphasis is on the apple, there is usually a little poiré - fermented pear juice - included into the mix to add a touch of elegance and finesse.

The best Calvados is produced in the lush orchards of the Auge Valley. The Calvados produced here is distinct for two reasons:
Firstly, it is the only Calvados with AOC - Appellation d'Origine Contrôlée - a system of quality control.

Secondly it is the only Calvados to be double distilled.

A Calvados that is single distilled can be identified by the words 'appelation réglementée'.

Calvados, sometimes affectionately referred to as 'Calva', is distilled from cider, aged and then finally blended. After fifteen years of ageing it takes on a smooth, dry persona with a scent of ripe apples.

When young Calvados is fiery and should be approached with some caution. Newcomers

The Spirits of Normandy.

should try it for taste first by dipping a sugar lump into the calvados. No need for embarrassment, the Normans do this too.

Unless you go for a VSOP or an XO example, Calvados tends to be relatively inexpensive.

Pommeau

This alcoholic drink is not particularly well-known outside France where it is drunk as an aperitif. Pommeau is a blend of freshly pressed cider apple juice and Calvados and aged in wooden barrels. It is very easy to drink - perhaps too easy - and makes a good companion for oysters or fois gras.

Bénédictine

Though not made from apples, this sweet liqueur is a thoroughly

French drink indegineous to Fécamp in Upper Normandy. It was originally made by a monk in 1510, and 3 centuries later was resecurrected by a successful wine and drinks merchant. He named the drink Bénédictine in memory of its monastic origins. It is made from a variety of aromatic herbs which grow locally on the cliffs. The drink contains 27 herbs but the exact recipe is a well guarded secret. The letters D.O.M which appear on the label stand for Deo Optimo Maximo - which means 'to God the best and the greatest'.

Pear Cider or Perry

This sparkling drink, known as poiré, is made from fermented pears. It is most popular in the wooded area North of Domfront in the Orne but not particularly well-known outside of France.

Eau, What A Choice!

It's the best thirst quenching drink there is. It's not alcohol but it's a bargain !

Mineral water, (eau minérale) both still (plate) and sparkling (gazeuse) is exceptionally good value for money and substantially cheaper to buy in France. Why this is so is perplexing as unlike alcohol, there is no tax to blame.

There is often a vast selection of different brands at the hyper-markets. Some, such as Evian, Volvic and the comparatively expensive Perrier will be familiar, yet some of the lesser known brands are just as good. In our blind tasting, we sampled some mineral waters at room temperature. Here are a selection of commonly available mineral waters:

Badoit: Slightly sparkling from the Loire.
Ave Price: FF3.50 (36p) 1L
Comment: Slightly salty
Contrexéville: From Vosges. Reputedly good for the kidneys. Has a slightly diuretic effect.
Ave Price: FF2.9 (30p) 1.5L
Comment: Slightly salty.
Evian: From the town of Evian at Lake Geneva.It has a slightly diuretic effect.
Ave Price: FF4.20 (43p) 2L
Comment: Tasteless but thirst quenching.
Perrier: A very well-marketed mineral water from Nîmes. Full of sparkle and is generally used as soda water in France.
Ave Price: FF4.5 (46p) 1L
Comment: Most refreshing with almost no flavour.
River: Sparkling water
Ave Price: FF1.75 (19p) 1.5L
Comment: Slightly chalky on the palate.
Vichy: A sparkler from Vichy.
Ave Price: FF3 (31p) 1.5L
Comment: Like bicarbonate of soda.
Vittel: A still yet rugged mineral water - from Nancy.
Ave Price: FF2.80 (30p) 1.5L
Comment: Refreshing and slightly sweet.
Volvic: A still water from Auvergne filtered through volcanic rock.
Ave Price: FF3 (31p) 1.5L
Comment: Smooth silky taste.

Tobacco Prices Up In Smoke!

With an average saving of £2.00 on a packet of cigarettes, topping up in France makes good financial sense.

Product	France	U.K.
Cigarettes	Av. £	Av. £
Benson & Hedges	£1.99	£3.99
Camel	£2.21	£3.99
Dunhill	£2.62	£3.99
Gauloises	£2.37	£3.99
Gitanes	£1.68	£3.99
John Player Special	£1.74	£3.25
Lambert & Butler	£2.15	£3.39
Marlboro	£2.25	£3.99
Philip Morris	£2.22	£3.99
Rothmans	£2.07	£3.99
Silk Cut	£2.25	£3.99
Superkings	£2.15	£3.85
Tobacco		
Drum 50g	£2.56	£7.80
Golden Virginia 40g	£2.00	£7.47
Old Holborn 40g	£2.25	£7.47
Samson 50g	£2.25	£7.37
Cigars x 5		
King Edward Imperial	£4.00	£8.90
Villager Export	£3.75	£4.60

It is interesting to note that a 20-cigarettes-a-day smoker would have to spend in the region of £1500 a year in the UK. In France the same outlay would be just £730. You can in theory buy unlimited amounts of tobacco for personal use both on board the ferries or in France but the 'advisory guideline' is 800. In France, tobacco can be purchased from outlets called Tabacs

These shops are similar to newsagents. Cigarette and tobacco prices are state regulated in France when sold through a tabac. This is not true of tobacco sold in cafés, bars and petrol stations where prices tend to be higher. Unlike the UK, French supermarkets do not sell tobacco at all. Most tabacs are closed on Sundays and bank holidays. Most accept sterling and credit cards.

The Epicurean's Tour of The Shops

When shopping in France the variety of traditional gastronomic shops give an insight into French life. It must be a cultural thing but very simply the French like to specialise.

Visit any French town and what stands out most is the array of specialist food shops, most of which do not have a UK counterpart.

Take the Boucherie for example - the butcher. The Boucherie sells all types of meat and poultry - except pork. To buy pork you need to visit the Charcuterie - which means cooked meat.

The Charcuterie, originally a pork butcher, has evolved into a pork based delicatessen. Visiting a Charcuterie for the first time will shift your perception of the humble pig 'le cochon' in gastro-nomic terms forever! Now you will see it as pâté, terrin, rillets, rillons, hams, dried sausages, fresh sausages, pieds de porc, andouillettes boudins noirs et blancs. This pork lovers haven also offers ready made pork meals with a selection of plats de jour that just need heating up.

Horse meat is also popular in France and this is sold at the Boucherie Chevaline - horse meat butcher, generally identifiable by a horse's head sign.

Cheese, a much revered commodity in France, is produced with exacting procedures by the highly skilled maître fromager (master cheese specialist). The shop to visit to really get the feel of the cheese culture at its best is the Fromagerie - a specialist cheese shop which will probably have around 300 varieties on sale.

A cross between a grocery store and delicatessen is the Epicerie. The store sells cheese and fresh meat amongst other food products. These days the Epricerie is based a little on the Supermarché and an Alimentation Général - a general store - and has lost its authenticity somewhat.

The Epicurean's Tour of The Shops

Dieppe and Le Havre both being fishing towns are awash with fresh seafood. You can buy the catch of the day from the Poissonerie. This could be a fishmonger or just a stall.

Another example of specialisation in action is the Boulangerie - the bakery. The shelves are stacked with all types of unusual bread and buns and occasionally cakes and quiches too.

But for a fiendishly good selection of cakes and biscuits, it is over to the Pâtisserie for specialist cake, flans and tarts. The Pâtisserie sometimes sells ice-cream too.

Sweets, not the commercial pre-wrapped type, but handmade sweets such as bon-bons, nougat and crystallised fruit, have their own home in a Confiserie or Chocolaterie - a high class sweet or chocolate shop. The products are a little pricey but good quality, delicious and beautifully packaged for you.

For fresh fruit, flowers and vegetables and a myriad of fresh French delights the best place is the Marché - outdoor market. These are generally open on a Saturday or Wednesday.

You could of course, by-pass the specialist shops which offer pleasant insightful echoes of French daily life and culture - a shopping experience unlike any you can have in the UK. You could, instead shop in one of the immense Hypermarché hypermarkets. The total anonymity that comes with being one of hundreds of trolley pushers walking around thousands of kilometres of floor space in a state of suspended reality is an experience all of its own!

Say Cheese

Take a glass of your favourite wine, break off a little baguette, fill it with your favourite cheese - Voila! a slice of French culture.

The inherent passion for wine within the French culture is closely followed by their love for cheese, so much so that France has become renowned for its remarkably large array of cheeses. Incredibly, the number of different varieties is believed to be in excess of 700. Not only do supermarkets dedicate large areas of floor space to their cheese counters, but the French also have specialist cheese shops.

These quaint shops are called 'Fromageries' (cheese shops) offering cheese in all its colours and consistencies.

Though nasal passages have to grapple with the pungent aroma that hangs heavily in the air, the palate can look forward to a delightful epicurean experience. It is at the fromagerie that the finest cheeses can be found,

thanks to the resident maître fromager (master cheese specialist). His highly skilled job combines the complexities of cheese selection, storage and the delicate process of **'affinage'**. This is the art of ageing a young cheese to maturity so that it is offered in its prime. This is especially important as some cheeses are seasonal and when out of season they are in fact out of date. A true cheese buff will know the right time of the year to buy them.

To the uninitiated though, the cheese counter must look like a daunting display of yellow and white hues with the odd shout of blue. No matter how tempting these colours look, one wonders about the taste. Fortunately, it is customary for supermarkets and fromageries to routinely offer **dégustation** (sampling) upon request.

Say Cheese

Although it is not possible to list all French cheeses, some may already be familiar such as the famous Camembert - and no wonder as there are over 2000 varieties.

Camembert is a soft cheese with a rind made up of moulds. The best has to be from Normandy, its birthplace, and more specifically from the area between the rivers Touques and Dives. Though the cheese was first made in 1791 by a local farm woman, the circular wooden box it now comes in was created by a Monsieur Ridel in 1905 so that the cheese could be exported. It was awarded an AOC in 1985. Look for the letters V.C.N (véritable Camembert de Normandie) for a farmhouse variety.

Fromages fermiers (farmhouse cheese) are considered to be the finest of all cheeses. These are made by small producers using milk from their own farm animals. When unpasteurised milk is used this is denoted with the words 'lait cru'. Other varieties to try are:

Bondard. Soft log shaped double-cream cheese with a fruity taste. The rind is a tan colour. Made from cows milk on farms. It is best in October/ November.

La Bouille. Hard, fruity drum shaped cheese made with double cream. Made in small dairies. Best in June and February.

Trappiste de Bricque-bec. Disc shaped mild cheese made by monks. It has an off-white rind.

Brillat-Savarin. This comes from Forges-les-Eaux, north of the Seine. Its triple cream content gives this cheese a 75% fat content. It is a soft and mild disc shaped cheese, with a downy white rind. It is in the group of cream cheeses under the Neufchâtel banner after the town of the same name. Records show that cheese was being made in the region of Neufchâtel since 1035. They are easy to spot in their varying heart, disc or obelisk shapes.

Say Cheese

Le Brin. This is a small hexagon shaped cheese. Made from cows' milk, it is mild and creamy. The edible rind has a delicate, pleasant aroma. The special method of production leaves the cheese high in calcium and phosphorus.

Cantorel Roquefort. A speciality of South-West France, this blue cheese is ripened in the caves of Cambalou for at least 90 days in accordance with its Appellation d'Origine Contrôlée. Made entirely from sheep's milk, its distinctive taste is best enjoyed with Barsac or Sauternes wines.

Livarot. This cheese was first made in the Vallée d'Auge in the small town of Livarot. It probably dates back to around 1690. It was granted an AOC in 1975. It is aged in airtight cellers lined with hay which probably contribute to its spicey, pungent aroma. It is characterised by its reddish-brown crust and a distinctive flavour.The term Colonel, refers to any of the five variations of Livarot.

Pont l'Evêque. This cheese has had a long history having been around since the 13th century. At that time it was produced by monks under the name of Angelot and in 1720 it won more acclaim further afield. It was was granted an AOC in 1976. It is square-shaped, small, soft, warm and tender with a gold rind. It is clean and pleasant, even fruity, on the palate. Best in summer, autumn and winter.

Pavé 'Auge. This is the term for the square cheeses of lower Normandy. Pont L'Evêque featured above, is one of these.

Rambol. Decorated with walnuts it looks like a small gateau.It is smooth with a mellow flavour.

Société Roquefort. Roquefort has been dubbed 'The King of Cheeses. Made exclusively from ewe's milk, it is creamy in texture and distinguished by its marbled green and ivory colouring. It has a mild piquant flavour.

The Neufchâtel Cheese Route

Dégustation - sampling - is the French way. Head for **Neufchâtel-en-Bray** taking the D1 from Dieppe. From there the route is signposted and leads to the south of the area.

At the dairies you can taste the subtle differences of the **Neufchâtel** cheese in its variety of forms - square, bond (cylindrical), double bonde, heart and large heart.

Serving suggestions:

- Cheese is at its best served at room temperature. Remove from the fridge at least one hour before required.
- Allow 2oz per person for a cheese board and 4oz per person for a cheese and wine evening.
- Select 3-4 different types of cheese for an attractive display, especially on a cheese board.

Storage Tips:

Fortunately, most hard cheeses are freezable as long as they are not overmature when frozen. This is not recommended for soft cheeses.

Generally, the following guidelines for fridge storage apply:

- Fresh Cheese (soft cheese) Eat within a few days.
- Blue Cheese Can be kept up to 3 weeks.
- Goats', Ewe's milk cheese will keep for up to two weeks.
- Always store cheese in the lowest part of the fridge wrapped in foil or in an air proof container to prevent drying out.

Fromagerie

French Bread

It's the law. Every French village must have its own boulangerie (bakery) supplying the villagers with freshly baked bread every day of the week.

Governed by French law, the boulangerie emerges as the single most important shop in any village, faithfully providing the villagers with an essential part of their staple diet - bread. As with all things French an etiquette has evolved around bread. It is generally considered unacceptable to serve bread purchased in the morning in the evening. No self respecting Frenchman would dare to insult his guests in this way. However, left over bread may be used perhaps for dunking into hot chocolate - in specially formulated wide cups - or alternatively can be cooked in soup.

The most famous and popular French bread (both within and outside France) is the long, thin baguette or French stick. It is uniform in length; and its weight - governed by French law - must be 250 grams!

Although the baguette is made simply from soft flour, yeast, water and a pinch or two of salt, it has an appealing fluffy texture and can be enjoyed just as well on its own as it can with food. However, its short life span means that it must be consumed soon after it has been baked. Bakeries routinely bake bread twice a day to ensure fresh bread for a very discriminating public.

Other extreme variations on the baguette are the ficelle (a word which literally

Boulangerie at the Hypermarket

French Bread

means string). It is the thinnest loaf available. In contrast un pain or Parisien is double the size of a baguette. A compromise is reached with petit pains and the bâtons which are much shorter than the baguette and similar to large rolls.

For breakfast (le petit dèjeuner) the French will also enjoy a Continental breakfast (better known in France as viennoisie). This includes such delicious treats as the famous pastry style croissant. This familiar crescent shaped roll was Marie Antoinett's inadvertent contribution to the Western breakfast culture. She introduced them to the Parisian Royals in the late 18th century where they proved to be an epicurean hit. In Marie Antoinette's home country of Vienna, however, the croissant had been making a regular appearance at the breakfast table as early as

1683. It was in this year that the Polish army saved the city from Turkish hands and in celebration the Viennese baked a crescent shaped creation based on the Ottoman flag - voila, the croissant was born!

The croissant is similar to puff pastry - made with yeast dough and butter and is usually accompanied by confit (crystallized fruit) or confiture (various flavours of jam). Sometimes it is served with jam, cheese or chocolate and can be savoured hot or cold.

Traditionally, the croissant is dunked by the French into their coffee in specially made wide cups designed for this purpose. This French idiosyncrasy can also be traced back to the late 17th century. The defeated Turks had left some sacks of coffee beans before they left Vienna. These were discovered by a group of

French Bread

Armenian Jews who started the croissant dunking tradition.

There are also many other tempting and unusual styles of bread available at the specialist boulangerie (bakery) or the boulangerie counter at the hypermarket.

Here are some suggestions you may like to try:

Pain au chocolat. a croissant style bun imbued with chocolate (delicious when warm but tricky as the chocolate seeps out).

Brioche. a breakfast bun made from yeast, dough, eggs and butter, giving it a wonderful sweet, buttery aroma and taste.

Couronnes. A baguette style bread in the shape of a ring.

Pain aux noix. An outstanding bread baked with walnuts on the inside and on the crust.

Pain aux olives. Bread with olives and olive oil.

Pain de sègle. Made with rye and wheat.

Pain noir. Wholemeal bread.

Pain de son. Wholemeal bread fortified with bran.

Pain de mie. Sliced bread with a soft crust. Used for sandwiches.

Pain biologique. This bread is baked with organic wholemeal flour.

Pain campagne. Flatter than baguettes but also heavier. They have the advantage of staying fresh for longer.

Pain au Levain/Pain à l'ancienne. Both these names refer to French bread made from sour dough. This is probably one of the oldest styles of French bread there is.

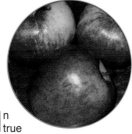

"An Apple A Day.... '
.....The Norman Way

I**n
true**
French style, even the last course of a meal is not the least. Dinner in any French home will always conclude with a sweet, which if not home made, will be bought from the Pâtisserie - a specialist cake shop. The Pâtisserie may also have a selection of handmade confectionery.

Like French wines and cheese, different areas of France have their own regional indulgences on offer and Normandy is no exception.

Normandy, blessed with a fertile land has, over the centuries, become famous for its apple orchards and its huge variety of apples. It is not surprising perhaps that there are so many types of apple pies.

Norman offerings include:

Tarte Normande
A simple apple pie.

Tarte aux pommes
Another type of apple pie - which is not so much a pie, more a tart with its pastry base topped with apple slices. It makes its appearance in a variety of shapes and sizes.

Gratin de Pommes Vallée D'Auge
No ordinary apple crumble; it is soaked in Calvados (an apple brandy produced in Normandy) and then baked in crème fraîche.

Chaussons aux pommes
An apple turnover.

Specialities at the Pâtisserie

Gâteau de Trouvilloe
A cake filled with cream and apples.

Bourdelots
This is translated as apple dumpling. It is pastry stuffed, with a baked apple.

Rabote
Baked apple in pastry.

Douillon
A pastry stuffed, with a whole baked pear.

Soufflé Normand
A souflé flavoured with apples and Calvados.

Sucre de Pommes
Apple sugar sticks.

Duchesses de Rouen
Macaroons

Teurgoule
Rice pudding Normandy style - a speciality of Houlgate. Thick, sweet, topped with caramel, flavoured with cinammon and baked slowly for hours in a cooling bread oven.

Mirlitons (de Rouen)
Small tarts filled with almond and cream.

Where to shop for your sweet tooth

La Fournil
174 Grande Rue, Dieppe
Tel: 00 33 35 82 74 77

Didier Cheron has revived an old Dieppoise tradition at his bakery - La Fournil. After the war 'etoiles de mer' star fish pastries were sold with  tea by a trader on his bike. Made simply with eggs, butter, flour and sugar they taste great and are only available at La Fournil. **If you buy a star Didier will give you 2 'chouquettes' (little balls made in the same way), FREE. Just show your guide.**

Pâtisserie Jeanne D'Arc
128 avenue Renée-Coty
Le Havre
Tel: 00 33 32 35 42 44 45

Heloin
89-100 rue des Carmes
Rouen
Tel: 00 33 32 35 71 02 94

Other Shopping Ideas

Drink and food are obvious shopping ideas in France. But there are other products which are cheaper or different and worth considering. The following pages give some guidance and tips to help you along the way.

TIP:
Serious bargain hunters should time their trip to France with the French sales. These happen twice a year - in January and in August and generally last between one to two months. You can pick up some fantastic bargains!

TIP:
Watch out! not everything is cheaper. Cat food, dog food, baked beans, tea bags tomato ketchup, sliced bread, margarine, tuna, frozen pizza, air freshener, nappies and most branded soap are actually more expensive to buy in France! Streaky bacon is almost double the price in France.
Amazingly Edam Cheese is more expensive in France.

Other Types of Shops on the High Street.

Alimentation Général
General Store.

Pharmacie
Chemist that sells primarily medicines.

Droguerie
Related to the hardware store, selling primarily toiletries.

Nettoyage à sec
Dry cleaners.

Carrelages
Sells tiles.

Tabac
Tobacconist, the only shop that sells cigarettes and tobacco. Also sells stamps.

Maison de la Presse
Sells magazines and newspapers

Librairie
Book shop

Quincaillerie:
Hardware store

Other Shopping Ideas

Chocolate Milkshake Drinks
The Nestlé Nesquick drinks are normally substantially cheaper in all French supermarkets - typically around £2.47 for 1 kilo. In the UK the standard 225gm Nesquick drink retails for around £1 (equivalent to £4 per kilo).This represents a 40% saving on the UK supermarket price.

Other French chocolate drinks worth trying are Goucao/Opticao 800g (at most supermarkets) which cost around FF9.45 and FF10.85 respectively. Prices compare favourably but they are also very tasty and a hit with the kids.

Chocolate - (Chocolat)
Chocolate making is a prosperous cottage industry and hand-made chocolates are quite a treat in France. The reduced prices are a treat for the Brits too.

Peanuts (Cacahuètes)
Look out for peanuts - 30% cheaper than the UK price!

Mustard (Moutard)
Mustard is substantially cheaper in France, and there is a wider selection. Dijon mustard prices start at FF1.75 (22p) for 370g jar of Dijon mustard compared to a typical UK price of 59p for 250g. English mustard is slightly hotter than its French counterparts. Try 'seeded' Dijon mustard; it has a particularly delicate flavour.

Anchovies- (Anchois)
You get a wider selection of anchovies, and at half price in France. They are particularly good value at the hypermarkets.

Kellogs Frosties
Frosties is one of the few breakfast cereals that is cheaper in France. Expect a 40% cheaper price tag.

Found a Bargain?
Don't keep it to yourself.
Write or email us and let us know.

Other Shopping Ideas

Olive Oil (Huile d'olives)
The finest French olive oils - like French wines - come from named origins and even *Appellations Controllées* - quality controlled areas similar to those of wine. They have a gentle flavour tempered with a slight sweetness and are great as condiments, but not suitable for cooking.

These olive oils have low acidity (sometimes as little as 0.2%) which is significant because acidity affects the rate at which the oil deteriorates.

Labels of assured finest quality to look out for are **'Huile de Provence'** and **'Huile d'Olives Nyons'** (the latter is subject to quality control with its own Appellation d'Origine. This sort of quality is expensive and could be up to £30.00 in the UK (less in France). Generally, you are likely to purchase brands that are commercially blended. Look for either Extra Virgin (Vierge) or First Cold Pressing (Premier Presson Froid) whose acidity is never more than 1%, but is better still at 0.5%, Fine Virgin olive oil at 1.5% or less, and Ordinary Virgin olive oil whose acidity level is 3%. This sort of quality olive oil in the UK is rarely below £6.00 per litre yet in France the price is around FF28.00 (£2.90).

Olives
In general olives (both black and green) are about 30% cheaper in the French Hypermarkets. They are great in a baguette with camembert and make a filling snack.

Rice - (Riz)
Rice, even Uncle Ben's is generally 30% cheaper in France. A 2kg pack of rice in the UK would on average be £2.85. The French equivalent would be around £1.99.

Cous Cous
Cous Cous is 50% less in France across the board.

Other Shopping Ideas

Coca Cola
A two litre bottle of coke is just under £1.00 in France. That's around 30% saving.

Schweppes Tonic Water
A 1.5L bottle of this tonic water is almost half price.

Orangina
A 2L bottle of oranina is about 30% cheaper.

Spirits
Most spirits are cheaper in France especially: Grants Gordons Gin and Smirnoff Vodka which are at least 30% cheaper.

Filtered Coffee -
(Café Moulu)
This is widely available and at half the UK prices. Try the taste of even the cheapest brands of filtered coffee and you will not be disappointed. A 1kg (4 x 250g pack) can be found for as little as FF29. Try Arabica. It is worth noting that these savings do not include instant coffee which costs the same.

TIP:
Take a cooler bag with you just in case you want to buy fresh products such as cheese or fish to maintain freshness and avoid any pungent smells on the journey home.

For the cooler bag

Butter
The label, President, is very popular in France and widely available in the UK. A quantity of 250gm costs just 52p in France which is almost half price.

Cheese
Camembert and Brie are probably the two most popular French cheese and both are at least 30% cheaper in France.

Fruit Juice (Jus de Fruit)
Expect to pay a third less. Brands such as Recre, Goldhorn and Lagona range from 29p-43p per 1L carton. The UK the price range would be 59-89p.

Fromage Frais Petit Filous
A pack of twelve is almost half price in France.

Other Shopping Ideas

Fish (Poisson)
If you have enjoyed a fish or seafood meal, you may be inclined to buy your own to take home. The hypermarkets generally have comprehensive fish and seafood sections or better still, you can visit a fish monger *(poissonnerie)*. You'll definitely need cooler bag!

Best for oysters
Goubert
Rue du 19 Août
Pourville-sur-Mer, nr Dieppe
Tel: 00 33 (0)235 84 36 20

Good for trout
Pisciculture de la Source
Rue des Basses-Terrest
Saint-Aubin-sur-Scie
nr Dieppe
Tel: 00 33 (0)235 85 42 88

Pisciculture
Chemin des Sondres
Montvillie, nr Rouen
Tel: 00 33 (0)235 33 71 74

Good for shellfish
Poissonerie Normonde
243 rue Aristide-Briand
Le Havre
Tel 00 33(0)235 41 24 93

Glassware
Duralex, Luminarc and Cristal D'Arques are names you may already be familiar with. They are available at the hypermarkets at prices that are at least 20% less than in the UK!

Baby's Furniture
Furniture for babies is always expensive, but considerably less in france:

Prams -	25% less
High chairs -	25% less
Bouncy chairs -	35% less
Travel cots -	50% less
Car seats -	55% less

Batteries
Around 20% cheaper in the hypermarkets.

Printers for the Computer
These tend to be 25-30% cheaper in France. For example a Hewlett Packard printer is £100.00 in France as opposed to £131.00 in the UK.

TIP:
If you are buying equipment for business you can claim back the French 20.6% VAT on your UK VAT form and save even more.

Other Shopping Ideas

Kid's Clothes
Stylish clothes for kids is easy to come by in France and usually less expensive than in the UK. For typically

Jacadi
specialists in stylish clothes for children and maternity wear

218 Grande Rue
Dieppe
Tel: 00 33 (0) 235 843 861
Closed Sunday & Monday

French style, try Jacadi. This stylish boutique is part of a chain, with shops all over the world, except for Britain. The make Jacadi is

an acknowledged quality brand abroad. They specialise in quality kids clothes from birth to 12 years alongside a range of beautiful maternity-wear all made from natural fibres. No polyester here!

Cellulite Cure!
Action Minceur is the brand name of cellulite curing tights. They claim that the tights massage away cellulite by releasing an algae type substance into your thighs as you walk. These are only available in France from good Pharmacies.

Mountain Bikes (VTT)
Adult mountain bikes start at under £100 and children's mountain bikes can be found for around £40. It is difficult to find these prices in UK.

Other Shopping Ideas

DECATHLON

Find your favourite sports at Decathlon,

cycling, fishing, tennis, camping, hiking, horse-riding, rollerskating, football, swimming, weights, golf...

High input
High
Fitness!

Ask for your FREE T-Shirt when you spend just FF300

Available in Dieppe & Le Havre.

valid on presentation of your guide.
1 per customer

The Number 1 sports store in Europe! A huge choice at low, low prices !

Be a Sport! Being a well-kitted sportsman is a pleasure; more so when you look at the price tag in France. The pound is strong at the moment so the price for most sports products in France compares well with prices in the UK.

The Decathlon sports hypermarket is really the only place to shop for sports gear. It sells an amazing range in every sports category for both amateurs and professionals - all the kit is here.

How To Get There:

Dieppe Branch
Val Druel, Tel: 0033 (0)231 14 41 41
Exit the port, take 2nd exit at roundabout. Cross over 2nd & 3rd roundabouts. At 4th roundabout take 3rd exit. At 5th roundabout turn right onto the Rouen road. Pass the Belvedere centre on left. After 500m turn right and follow road to the left.

Le Havre Branch, ZAC des Deux Rivières, Montivilliers
Tel: 0033 (0)232 79 26 26
Exit the port, 2nd exit at roundabout. right at lights. Follow Toutes Directions sign. Stay on right lane through the lights to take exit signed Montivilliers. Stay on the left to follow signs to Montivilliers then Montivilliers La Lezarde, then Centre Commercial. Take left exit.

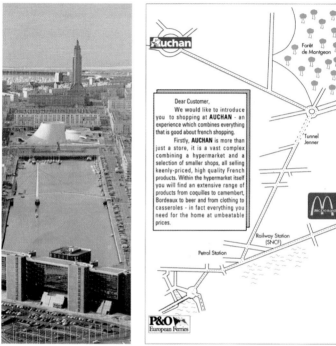

Dear Customer,

We would like to introduce you to shopping at **AUCHAN** - an experience which combines everything that is good about french shopping.

Firstly, **AUCHAN** is more than just a store, it is a vast complex combining a hypermarket and a selection of smaller shops, all selling keenly-priced, high quality French products. Within the hypermarket itself you will find an extensive range of products from coquilles to camembert, Bordeaux to beer and from clothing to casseroles - in fact everything you need for the home at unbeatable prices.

Phototechnic Le Havre

WELCOME TO AUCHAN LE HAVRE

Open from Monday to Saturday
from 8.30 until 22.00
Petrol Station open 24 hours a day

LE HAVRE
Guarded car-park

☎ 02 35 54 71 71

Other Shopping Ideas

Pots & Pans
You may already be familiar with the names 'Le Creuset' and 'Tefal'. These two popular quality brands of pots and pans are both manufactured in France. You can purchase these in the French hypermarkets and supermarkets for as little as half the UK price. For example, the Le Creuset 20cm saucepan is typically sold in the UK for around £33.00 yet it is available at French hypermarkets at around FF127 (£15.50).

Tissues
Both boxed and handbag size are at least 25% cheaper across the board.

Garden Furniture (Jardinage)
Garden furniture is often half the UK price of the equivalent and tempting to buy - but you will need a lot of space in your car! At Leroy Merlin (next to Auchan), Continent, Carrefour and Auchan, there is a good selection of both plastic and pine table and chair sets. Plastic chairs start from FF19.95 (£2.50) and plastic tables 85cm in diameter from as little as FF119.00 (£14.90). A pine table and chair set can be found for only FF599.00 (£75.00).

Garden parasols are also around £10.00 cheaper in France.

Light Bulbs
Not a huge saving to be made, but 15% is enough to bring a little light.

TIP:
Most shops close at lunch time usually between 12 noon and 2pm. This does not apply to the hypermarkets.

Check Out the Automatic Check-Inns

If you are looking to stay overnight or longer on a budget then any of France's budget hotels may be a good option. For these hotels, functionality is the primary concern, so no room service, luxurious towels, beautiful furniture or scenic views. But they are usually situated close to the motorway networks, so you can check-in and out and be back on route with ease.

These hotels operate on an unmanned auto-check-in basis. Entrance is by credit card through a 'hole in the wall' using the language of your choice, and you have 24 hour access. The rooms are clean, functional and usually comprise a double and a single bed (bunk) plus a colour TV.

The Formule 1 hotel is cheap at around £19 per night for up to 3 people but the shower and toilet is communal - most annoying if you get into the shower only to find you have forgotten the soap! Worse, still if you get back to your room to find you have forgotton the entry code!

Restaurants are never part of the internal landscape of a budget hotel, but there is a snack vending machine which is always accessible. In the morning a simple Continental breakfast, though not cordon bleue, is good value for money at around £2.50 per person.

BUDGET HOTELS IN FRANCE

Name	Room price from FF	Beds/ room	Central Reservation
B&B	160	4	00 33 2 98 33 75 00
Bonsai	149	3	00 33 1 42 46 15 45
Formula 1	119	3	00 33 8 36 68 56 85
Mister Bed	149	4	00 33 1 46 14 38 00

The majority of hotels are one and two star hotels and prices tend to vary depending on location and comfort. The chain hotels can generally be relied upon to deliver a good quality of service within their star rating. For instance, you can expect a TV, telephone and an en-suite shower room as part of the package in a two star hotel. A bathroom would cost more.

Chambres d'hotes are becoming popular in France. These are French style bed and breakfasts, mostly run by ordinary people who have turned their private homes into touristic accommodation. They tend to be cheaper than hotels and give a flavour of French life, and character. Breakfast tends to be just a coffee, bread or croissant and maybe cheese. These days, many B&B signs offer an English breakfast and is testament to the increasing number of English visitors.

A gîte - country lodging - situated in the countryside gives a feeling of rural living. The kind of accommodation ranges from a simple room or perhaps an entire house. Contact Gîtes de France for more information on Tel: 00 33 1 47 42 20 20.

Château's also make for beautiful retreats and are often old castles or country mansions.

1 & 2 STAR HOTEL CHAINS IN FRANCE	
Tariffs vary between £20-£60 per room	
Name	Central Reservation
Balladins *	00 33 1 64 46 49 00
Campanile - Motel style	00 33 1 64 62 46 46
Ibis-Arcade **	00 33 1 69 91 05 63
Logis de France * / ** / ***	00 33 1 45 84 83 84

Hotels in Dieppe
Best choice of hotels are
situated on boulevard de
Verdun overlooking the sea.

Les Arcades **
1-3 arcades de la Bourse
Dieppe
Faces the port
Tariff: From FF260
Tel: 00 33 235 84 14 12

Hotel Aguado***
30 boulevard de Verdun
Dieppe
Overlooks the sea. Breakfast
is in a quiet lounge.
Tariff: From FF230
Tel: 00 33 235 84 27 00

L'Eolienne
30 rue de la Croix de Pierre
Rouxmesnil, 2km from
Dieppe, in a restored barn.
Tariff: From FF220
Tel: 00 33 235 84 53 75

Ibis**
rue de la vieille grange
Val Druel, Dieppe
Tariff: From FF285
Tel: 00 33 235 82 14 47

Hôtel de la Jetée
5 rue de l'asile Thomas
Dieppe
Faces the sea opp Cité de la mer
Tariff: FF150
Tel: 00 33 235 84 89 98

Hôtel de la Plage**
20 boulevard de Verdun
Dieppe
Near the Château
Tariff: From F260
Tel: 00 33 235 84 18 28

Hôtel-Restaurant Pointoise
10 rue Thiers, Dieppe
Nr the SNCF railway
Tariff: From FF150
Tel: 00 33 235 84 14 57

Hôtel Présidence***
boulevard de Verdun
Dieppe
Situated below the château
at the end of the seafront.
Dismal grey exterior, but
well-equipped & roof-top
restaurant.
Tariff: From FF280
Tel: 00 33 235 84 31 31

Hôtel Tourist*
16 rue de la Halle au Blé
Dieppe
Converted town house,
behind Casino
Tariff: From FF135. En suite
showers extra
Tel: 00 33 235 06 10 10

Hôtel Windsor**
18 boulevard de Verdun
Dieppe, Faces the sea
Tariff: From FF150. Extra for
seaview rooms.
Tel: 00 33 235 84 15 23

Hotels in Fécamp

Hôtel l'Admiral***
15 quai Vicomté
Fécamp
Tariff: From FF290
Tel: 00 33 235 10 01 00

Hôtel de l'Angleterre**
91-93 rue de la Plage
Fécamp
Slightly back from the sea.
Owned by an English family.
Has its own Restaurant &
English pub
Tariff: From FF250
Tel: 00 33 235 28 01 60
Special offer: A **FREE** Kir
Normand with your meal in
the restaurant or a **FREE**
glass of Bulldog (draught
beer) in the pub. Just show
your guide.

Ferme de la Chappelle***
Côte de la Vierge
Fécamp
Tariff: From From FF315
Tel: 00 33 235 10 12 12

Hôtel de la Plage**
87 rue de la Plage
Fécamp
Close to beach - no sea view,
quiet and comfortable
Tariff: From 230
Tel: 00 33 235 29 76 51

Hotels in Etretat

Hôtel le Donjon***
Chemin de Saint Clair
Etretat
Lovely château
Tariff: From FF580
Tel: 00 33 235 27 08 23

Hôtel l'Escale**
Place Foch
Etretat
Simple and pleasant
Tariff: From FF290
Tel: 00 33 235 27 03 69

Hôtel les Falaises**
1 boulevard du Président
Coty, Etretat
Tariff: From FF190
Tel: 00 33 235 27 02 77

Hôtel La Résidence**
4 boulevard du Président
Coty, Etretat
Lovely half timbered facade
Tariff: From FF170
Tel: 00 33 235 27 02 87

Hôtel St Christophe
Le Tilleul
3 km south of Etretat. Use
D940 road to get to the
chalet set back from Le
Havre road
Tariff: From FF280
Tel: 00 33 235 28 84 19

Hotels

Hotels in Le Havre

Hôtel de Bordeaux***
147 rue Louis Brindeau
Le Havre
Part of Best Western Chain.
Situated north side of
Espace Oscar Niemeyer,
facing the Volcano.
Tariff: From FF400
Tel: 00 33 235 22 69 44

Hôtel Celtic**
106 rue Voltaire
Le Havre
Overlooking Espace Oscar
Niemeyer and the Volcano
Tariff: From FF195
Tel: 00 33 235 42 39 77

Hôtel Faidherbe*
21 rue du Général Faidherbe
Le Havre
Family hotel near ferry port
Tariff: From FF110
Tel: 00 33 235 42 20 27

Hôtel Jeanne dArc*
19 Emile-Zola, Le Havre
Tiny, basic hotel
Tariff: From FF135
Tel: 00 33 235 21 67 27

Hôtel le Monaco**
16 rue de Paris, Le Havre
On a lively corner facing the
quay. Convenient for ferries
Tariff: From FF140
Tel: 00 33 235 42 21 01

Grand Hôtel Parisien**
1 cours de la République
Le Havre
Situated opposite the SNCF
railway
Tariff: From FF180
Tel: 00 33 235 25 23 83

Hôtel Richelieu
132 rue de Paris
Le Havre
Tariff: From FF160
Tel: 00 33 235 42 38 71

Hôtel Séjour Fleuri*
71 rue Emile Zola
Le Havre
Conveniently close to the
ferry terminal
Tariff: From FF110
Tel: 00 33 235 41 33 81

Hôtel Vent D'Ouest***
4 rue de Caligny
Le Havre
Situated near the entrance to
the St-Joseph church. Just
follow the tower to get there.
The rooms are well-
decorated with a nautical
theme, comfortable and have
a tv and ensuite shower or
bath. Service is friendly and
generally good.
Tariff: From FF410
Tel: 00 33 235 42 50 69
Special offer: A welcome
drink for Channel Hoppers

Hotels

Hotels in Rouen

Hôtel Beauséjour
9 rue Pouchet
Rouen - Near the station
Tariff: From FF150
Tel: 00 33 235 71 93 47

Hôtel Bristol
45 rue aux Juifs
Rouen
Overlooks Palais de Justice.
Nine rooms, all en-suite
Tariff: From FF200
Tel: 00 33 235 71 54 21

Hôtel Cardinal**
1 Place de la Cathédrale
Rouen
Great location opposite the
cathedral. Rooms en-suite.
Tariff: From FF250
Tel: 00 33 235 70 24 42

Hôtel des Carmes**
33 place des Carmes
Rouen
Pretty hotel in quiet square
Tariff: From FF210
Tel: 00 33 235 71 92 31

Hôtel de la Cathédrale
12 rue St-Romain
Rouen
Near cathedral. Very nice
courtyard. Parking a
problem. Tariff: From FF250
Tel: 00 33 235 71 57 95

Hôtel de Dieppe***
Place Bernard Tissot
Rouen
Opposite station. Part of
Great Western chain
Tariff: From FF350
Tel: 00 33 235 71 96 00

Hôtel des Familles*
4 rue Pouchet
Rouen
Opposite station
Tariff: From FF150
Tel: 00 33 235 71 88 51

Hôtel Frantour Vieux Marché
33 rue du Vieux Palais
Rouen
Modern hotel. Near Place du
Vieux Marché
Tariff: From FF350
Tel: 00 33 235 71 00 88

Hôtel de Lisieux
4 rue de la Savonnerie
Rouen
Between the river and the
cathedral
Tariff: From FF150
Tel: 00 33 235 71 87 52

Hôtel du Quebec**
18 rue Québec
Rouen
Tariff: From FF170
Tel: 00 33 235 70 09 38

Take a herd of saucy Norman cows, an apple and pear orchard, and the fruits of the sea and voila!
Norman Gastronomy

Norman cooking is most distinctive and not advisable for the calorie conscious. Often double or even triple cream is used to enrich sauces embuing the food with that unmistakable taste of Normandy.

Norman cuisine is a challenge for the body and what's more the French eat a lot of it. Around 400 years ago a custom began to aid digestion. Unlike the Romans who practiced bulimia, the Normans preferred to aid digestion by creating a little hole 'trou' in the stomach by drinking a glass of Calvados in between the first and second course. If you are on a gourmet adventure, try it and enjoy.

The cow and its many ensuing dairy products together with the apple, cider and calvados appear in most recipes. The most popular sauce is the thick yellow **Sauce Normande**, a whisked mixture of cream and butter added to a cider sauce. It is used routinely to cover practically everything from fish to vegetables.

Apart from yielding its fruit, the sea tends to flood the pastures of Normandy leaving behind its salt on the grass. This greatly influences the flavour of the grazing lambs. The resulting dish is known as **Angeau Pré-Salé,** ready salted lamb!

The Norman cow is distinguished by its brown 'eye patches'

***Everything stops
for lunch in France.
Take time out to enjoy a pastime the
French take very seriously -
eating!***

You know lunchtime has arrived in France when you see the sign **'fermé'** (closed) on shop doors. As the shops and factories close, the restaurants open for business, offering a choice of cuisine and ambience.

French culinary diversity is very much inspired by France's variety of landscape and locally farmed produce and Normandy is no exception.

Generally three distinct styles of cuisine are evident:

Haute Cuisine
The hallmarks of Haute Cuisine is its rich food and elaborate presentation.

This style can be tracked back to Louis XIV's twelve hour feasts in the palace of Versailles.

Bourgeoise Cuisine
This style is related to Haute Cuisine. Less elaborate perhaps and best described as high quality home cooking. Well known dishes in this category would be 'coq au vin' and 'boeuf à la bourguignonne', perhaps the French version of 'meat and two veg'!

Nouvelle Cuisine
This trendy cooking style originated in the 1970's. The dishes are generally less rich, fresh ingredients are used and vegetables

'The Norman Hole' a 400 year old custom of preparing the stomach for a big meal - wash down the first course with a glass of Calvados are el dente - almost raw to optimise their natural flavours and aromas. The trouble is, though the food is great, it is not very filling.

Choosing a restaurant is easy as they generally display their menus outside. Steer clear of empty restaurants - in our experience, if a restaurant remains unpopulated by 12.30pm, they generally deserve to be so! If you have not eaten by 3pm, then you will find yourself stumped for choice as most restaurants close by 3pm. The only option is a café or a brasserie where drinks are served and a limited selection of sandwiches are available. Creperies are another option as they tend to stay open most of the day as are the fast food chains.

If you have booked a table be sure to be on time, as your table is unlikely to be saved for more than ten minutes. This is especially true on Sundays. The French have a sense of specialness about Sundays. Though lunch is the main meal of any day, on this day, lunch is a gastronomic occasion when everyone likes to eat out 'en famille'. These meals tend to last around 3 hours. It is worth noting that in most French restaurants, the cheapest set menu meal is not available on Sundays - or on public holidays

Everything has its time and place and that includes lunchtime.
In France lunch is strictly between **12pm - 3pm**

Most restaurants cater for the tourists by offering a **'menu touristique'** usually written in English or with an English translation, alongside the regional dishes. This is usually good value for money and comprises such dishes as steak and French fries, or perhaps an omelette or simple fish dish; these dishes tend to be associated with the British. Not all prices will be highlighted on the menu. The letters **SG** may sit alongside some dishes and stand for '**selon grosseur**' (according to weight). This applies to dishes that, for practical purposes, are sold by weight, such as lobster or fish. In this instance it is advisable to find out the price before you order.

In France the word 'sandwich' means a filled baguette. Sliced bread is a British thing!

One item that will be missing from any French menu is the traditional two-slices-of-bread British sandwich. You may find the word 'sandwich' referred to on the menu at cafés or brasseries, but it will never be served in sliced bread. The most popular 'sandwich' is the **croque monsieur** which is basically ham and cheese in a toasted **ficelle** (a slimmer version of a baguette). The feminine version of this - **croque-madame** - is served garnished with a fried egg. Alternatively, you could choose the **Prix Fixé** menu, a set price menu which may include the **plat du jour** (dish of the day) or **spécialité de la maison** (house special). These are a better choice for those wishing to try a local dish, usually seafood or frogs legs - 'cuisses de grenouilles'. Indulge in the **à la carte** menu or the **menu gastronomique** for finer quality and therefore more expensive food.

If the words **service compris** (service included) or **service et taxes compris** (service & taxes included) or simply the abbreviation **s.c.** are on the menu, that means the prices include taxes and a service charge. However, odd coins are usually left for the waiter. Otherwise, a 10% tip is customary.

Meals are never rushed in restaurants even if you only want a snack and a drink at one of the cafés. You can wile away the time at your leisure but if your are eating to a deadline, pay for your meal when it arrives, as catching the waiter's eye later may prove a challenge!

Well Done or Raw?

Be precise when ordering your meat dish. The French like theirs quite rare. So if your like your meat pink then take it as it comes.

Otherwise be sure to specify in the following way:

bleu	very rare
saignant	rare
à point	medium rare
bien cuit	medium
bien bien cuit	well done

The last phrase is a little tongue in cheek and likely to be used only by the British, as the French never eat their meat this way. Nevertheless it sends the message to the chef.

Restaurant Etiquette

To get the attention of the waiter

DO
Lift your index finger and call **Monsieur**

A waitress should be addressed as **Madam** or if she is very young, **Madmoiselle**.

Alternatively just say **'s'il vous plaît'.**

DO NOT
Call a waiter garçon. This will be regarded as an insult and a sure way of receiving bad service.

DO NOT
Snap your fingers or clap your hands at the waiter. You will be ignored.

DO NOT
Do not ask for a 'doggy-bag'. This concept simply does not exist in France.

Treat Your Tastebuds

Go for French food while in France. This not only adds to the French experience, but also makes good economic sense; traditional British food and drink such as tea, Scotch whisky and gin or a plate of bacon and eggs are expensive. So check out the menu or **'tarif des consommations'** (if in a café or bar) for something that tickles your palate and accompany it with wine (vin ordinaire) or draught beer (pression).

Alternatively French spirits and soft drinks are generally an inexpensive relative to their British counterparts on the menu.

Coffee?

When ordering coffee, be specific and say exactly what you would like. Unlike British restaurants, just ordering a coffee will not do because the French have a different idea of how a standard coffee should be served. They will routinely serve it strong and black, espresso style. The exception to this is during the breakfast meal when coffee is served in large wide-mouthed coffee cups - specially designed for dunking - and hot milk is a standard accompaniment.

Coffee Styles

Un café, s'il vous plaît
You will receive an espresso coffee, strong and black in a small espresso cup

Un café au lait, s'il vous plaît
You will receive an espresso coffee with milk on the side.

Une crème s'il vous plaît
You will receive a small white coffee

Une crème grande s'il vous plaît
You will receive a white coffee served in normal size cup.

Menu Terms

Les Viandes — **Meat**

L'agneau	Lamb
Assiette Anglaise	Plate of cold meat
Bifteck	Steak
Bifteck haché	Hamburger
Boeuf	Beef
Boudin Noir	Black pudding
Contrefilet	Sirloin
Entrecôte	Steak
Foie	Liver
Foie gras	Goose liver
Faux filet	Sirloin Steak
Jambon	Ham
Langue	Tongue
Porc	Pork
Rognons	Kidneys
Saucisse	Sausage

Volaille — **Poultry**

Canard	Duck
Cimier	Venison
Dindon	Turkey
Oie	Goose
Faisan	Pheasant
Perdreau	Partridge
Pigeon	Pigeon
Poulet	Chicken(roast)
Poulet boivin	Sauteed chicken
Poularde	Chicken (boiled)
Poussin	Spring chicken

Sauce — **Sauce**

Béarnaise	Sauce from egg yolks, shallots, wine & tarragon
Béchamel	White sauce with herbs
Beurre blanc	Loire sauce with butter, wine & shallots
Beurre noir	Blackened butter
Bouillade	Sauce of sweet peppers, garlic & wine for snals or fish
Meunière	Butter & lemon sauce

Divers — **Miscellaneous**

Braisé	Braised
Brochette	Skewer
Brouillade	Stew with oil
Brouillé	Scrambled
Canapé	Small filled pasty/bread snack or starters
Cuit au four	Baked
Fumé	Smoked
Gratinée	Grill browned
Grillé	Grilled
Poivre	Pepper
Rôti	Roast
Sel	Salt
Suprême	Chicken breast or game bird
Terrine	Coarse paté

Fish dishes are a speciality of any fishing port, especially of Dieppe and Le Havre.

Les Poissons	Fish
Amande	Clams
Anchois	Anchovy
Anguille	Eel
Araignée de mer	Spider crab
L'Assiette de fruits de mer	Sea food platter
L'Assiette Nordique	Smoked fish platter
Bar	Bass
Baudroie	Monkfish
Brème	Bream
Calamar	Squid
Coquilles	Scallops
Crevette grise	Shrimp
Crevette rose	Prawn
Crustacés	Shellfish
Escargots	Snails
Flétan	Halibut
Fruit de mer	Seafood
Gamba	Large prawn
Haddock	Smoked haddock

note: aiglefin is the name for fresh haddock

Hareng	Herring
Homard	Lobster
Huître	Oyster
Limand	Lemon sole
Moules	Mussels
Royan	A type of large sardine
Saumon	Salmon
Saumon fumé	Smoked salmon
Saumonette	Sea eel or dog fish
Sausson	A paste mix of anchovy, almonds, olive oil & mint spread on bread
Thon	Tuna
Truite	Trout
Truite arc en ciel	Rainbow trout

NormanSpecialities

Andouilles de Vire
Smoked pork and tripe
served cold as a starter.

Boudin blanc
Thick white sausage made of
chick or white meat.

Boudin Noir
Black pudding, sausage
made with pig's blood

Caneton à la rouennaise
Stuffed roasted duck served
with a rich sauce fortified with
blood.

Ficelle normande
Ham and cheese pancake or
mushrooms in creamy sauce.

Filet mignon de porc
normande
Pork tenderloin-cooked with
apples and onions in cider,
served with caramilzed apple.

Jambon au cidre
Ham baked in cider

Marmite dieppoise
Mixed fish soup with white
wine, leeks and cream

Moules à la marinière
Mussels in white wine and
shallots.

Moules à la normande
Mussels in a white wine and
cream sauce.

Omelette Mère Poulard
Named after the inventor,
who has a restaurant on
Mont St Michel. Light,
spongy because the whites
and yolks are beaten
separately before mixing.

Omelette normande
Omelette with mushrooms,
cream, Calvados and
shrimps or perhaps apples.

Pieds de mouton à la
rouennaise
Stuffed sheeps trotters - can
be grilled or fried.

Poulet/veau Vallee d'Auge
Chicken/veal cooked in cider
and Calvados with cream
and apples.

Salade cauchoise or
normande
Potatoes, celery and ham
salad in a cream dressing.

Eating Out - the Menu

Sole à la Dieppoise
Sole cooked in a white wine,
cream and mushroom sauce

Sole Normonde
Dover sole in cider and
cream served with shrimps

Tord-goule or tergoile
Rice pudding flavoured with
cinnamon

Tripes à la de Caen
Slow cooked trie with herbs
in cider and Calvados

Tripes de la Ferté-Macé
Tripe slow-cooked on skewers

Are you a vegetarian?
Unfortunately, Normandy
does not cater well for
vegetarians. Crêperies
may be a solution or
perhaps an omelette dish.

A useful phrase to say to a
sympathetic waiter:
Je suis végétarien(ne)
il y a quelques plats sans
viande?

I am a vegetarian. Are
there any non-meat
dishes?

Confused?

Some items on a menu look very similar but are in fact very different. Take in this list of to avoid inadvertently ordering something unappealing.

aiguillette	thin slice of meat
anguillette	tiny eel
brochet	pike
brochette	skewered food
cervelas	a type of sausage
cervelle	brain
gras	fat
gras double	Ox tripe
ris	sweetbreads
riz	rice
sauce tartare	mayonnaise sauce
steak tartare	raw steak

Specialities of Dieppe

Seafood and 'fruit de la mer' are prevalent in Dieppe. These include scallops (Dieppe is renowned for having the largest scallop bed in the Channel), sole and whiting.

The dish **La Marmite Dieppoise** is very popular. It is a fish stew made with local mussels, turbot, sole, langoustines, scallops and angler fish.

Cider is a very popular drink in these parts.

Restaurants of Dieppe

L'Armorique
17 quai Henri IV
Dieppe
Tel: 00 33 (0)235 84 28 4
Tariff: From approx.FF70
Cuisine: Seafood & café
Closed: Sun pm & Mon

L'Ancrage
9 arcades de la
Poissonnerie
Dieppe
Tel: 00 33 235 84 21 45
Tariff: From FF59
Cuisine: Seafood
Closed: Wed.

Les Arcades
1 Arcades de la Bourse
Dieppe
Tel: 00 33 235 84 14 12
Tariff: From FF79
Cuisine: Seafood
Open: daily

Comptoir Deep
Place Camille St. Saens
Dieppe
Tel: 00 33 235 06 09 11
Tariff: From Ff78
Cuisine: Traditional
Closed: Mon & Jan.

Les Ecamias
129 quai Henri-IV
Dieppe
Tel: 00 33 235 84 67 67
Tariff: From FF68
Cuisine: Regional dishes
Closed: Sun pm & Mon

flunch

RESTAURANT

OPEN 7/7 11.00 am to 10.00 pm

C.C. Auchan
DIEPPE

L'Eolienne
30 rue de la Croix de
Pierre, Dieppe
Tel: 00 33 (0)235 84 53 75
Tariff: Various
Cuisine: Norman dishes
Open: Daily

La Musardière
61 quay Henri IV, Dieppe
Tel: 00 33 (0)235 82 94 14
Tariff: From FF84
Cuisine: Fish and seafood
Excellent Dieppoise
cooking
Closed: Mon.

Flunch
Centre Commercial du
Belvedere
Attached to Auchan
Tariff: Various
Cuisine: Informal

Marmite Dieppoise
8 rue St Jean, Dieppe
Tel: 00 33 (0)235 84 24 26
Tariff: From FF83
Cuisine: Seafood - local
speciality of heaped bowls
with mixed seafood.
Closed: Sun & Thurs pm,
Mon & mid Nov-Mid Dec

Dieppe contd.

Brasserie - Restaurant
Le Festival
11 quai Henri IV, Dieppe
Situated by the Port de
Plaisance .
Tel: 00 33 (0)235 40 24 29
Tariff: From FF55
Cuisine: Seafood
Open: Daily all year
English spoken and
sterling accepted.
Special Offer: A **FREE**
glass of Champagne for
Channel Hoppers when
you show your guide.

Méli Mélo
55 quai Henri IV, Dieppe
Tel: 00 33 (0)235 06 15 12
Tariff: From FF39
Cuisine: Mix & Snacks

Le New Haven
53 quai Henri-IV, Dieppe
Tel: 00 33 (0)235 84 89 72
Tariff: From FF89
Cuisine: Norman dishes

Le Sully
92 quai Henri-IV, Dieppe
Tel: 00 33 (0)235 84 23 13
Tariff: From FF75
Cuisine: Seafood
Closed: Tues night & Wed

Café des Tribunaux
place du Puits Salé,
Dieppe
Tel: 00 33 (0)235 84 17 70
Tariff: Various
Cuisine: Popular bar &
brasserie with a smoke-
filled atmosphere, but it is
a focal point square.

La Tourelles
43 rue du Commandant
Fayolle, Dieppe
Tariff: From FF68
Cuisine: Known for
paellas.
Closed: Mon

La Voute
27 rue des Cordiers
Dieppe
Tel: 00 33 (0)235 40 13 44
Tariff: FF50
Cuisine: Crepes & Salads

Restaurants of Veules-Les-Roses

Les Galets
3 rue Victor Hugo
Veules-Les-Roses
Tel: 00 33 (0)235 97 61 33
Tariff: From FF160
Cuisine: French
Closed: Tues pm & Wed

Specialities of Fécamp
Fécamp is known for its particularly good cod and mackerel dishes. Wash it down with the local spirit - Benedictine.

Restaurants of Fécamp

La Marée
75 quai Bérigny
Fécamp
Tel: 00 33 (0)235 29 39 15
Tariff: From FF98
Cuisine: Fish & shop too
with harbour views
Closed: Sun pm & Mon

La Marine
23 quai de la Vicomté
Fécamp
Tel: 00 33 (0)235 28 15 94
Tariff: From FF70
Cuisine: Fish

Le Grand Banc
63 quai Bérigny
Fécamp
Tel: 00 33 (0)235 28 28 68
Tariff: From FF68
Cuisine: Fish mainly
Closed: Thurs

La Plaisance
quai Vicomte
Fécamp
Tel: 00 33 (0)235 29 38 14
Tariff: From FF130
Cuisine: Fish
Closed Tues/Wed pm

Restaurants of Etretat

Le Gallon
Boulevard Réné Coty
Etretat
Tel: 00 33 235 29 48 74
Tariff: From FF115
Cuisine: Seafood
Closed: Thurs lunch/Wed

L'Huitriière
place du Général de
Gaulle, Etretat
Nr. steps of Falais d'Aval
Tel: 00 33 235 27 02 82
Tariff: From FF115
Cuisine: Seafood in a 1st
floor panoramic dining
room.

Le Normandie
Place Maréchal-Foch
Etretat
Tariff: From FF98
Tel: 00 33 235 27 06 99
Cuisine: Fish

Specialities of Le Havre
Check out the herring **à la Havrais**..

Restaurants of Le Havre

La Petite Auberge
32 rue de Ste Adresse
Le Havre
Tel: 00 33 235 46 27 32
Tariff: From FF118
Cuisine: Traditional
Closed: Sun pm & Mon.

Petit Bedom
37 rue Louis Brindeau
Le Havre
Near to the Volcano
Tel: 00 33 235 41 36 81
Tariff: From FF155
Cuisine: French in a
Sophisticated atmosphere
Closed Sat lunch & Sun

Le Bistro des Halles
7 place des Halles-
Centrales, Le Havre
Tel: 00 33 235 22 50 52
Tariff: From FF42
Cuisine: Bistro/wine bar

L'Huitrière
12 quai Michel Féré
Le Havre
Faces the rotating bridge
Tel: 00 33(0) 235 21 24 16
Tariff: From FF91
Cuisine: Seafood fare

Tilbury
39 rue Jean-de-la
Fontaine, Le Havre
Tel: 00 33 (0)235 21 23 50
Tariff: From FF90
Cuisine: Emphasis on
baked dishes. Unusual
Closed: Sun pm & Mon

Le Winch
1 Quai Southampton
Le Havre
Tel: 00 33 (0)235 41 75 18
Tariff: From FF58
Cuisine: Seafood

Yves Page
27 place Georges-
Clemenceau, Ste Adrese
Tel: 00 33 (0)235 46 06 09
Tariff: From FF100
Cuisine: Seafood. Nice
views
Closed: Sun pm & Mon

Specialities of Rouen

Duck is a very popular dish. **Caneton à la Rouennaise**, is a typical dish: roast duckling stuffed with liver and served in a creamy stock and blood sauce. **Canard à la Duclair** is similar but simpler. Chicken from this area is also considered highly.

For dessert try Rouen's other culinary speciality: **Sucre de Pomme - apple sticks.**

Restaurants of Rouen

North of the square is abundant with Tunisian takeaways.

Bistrot d'Adrien
37 place du Vieux Marché
Rouen
Tel:00 33 (0)235 71 57 73
Tariff: From FF78
Cuisine: Traditional and simple. The building is old and full of character.There are three rooms each with a different ambience.

Au Temps des Ceries
4 rue des Basnage
Rouen
Tel:00 33 (0)235 89 98 00
Tariff: From FF60
Cuisine: Cheese dishes.
Closed Mon. lunch & Sun.

Le Beffroy
15 rue du Beffroy, Rouen
Tel:00 33 (0)235 71 55 27
Tariff: From FF100
Cuisine: Typically Norman
Closed: Sun pm.

Brasserie de la Grande Poste
43 rue Jeanne d'Arc.
Rouen
Tel:00 33 (0) 35 70 08 70
Tariff: From FF40
Cuisine: Brasserie style - just a coffee or full dinner.

La Butte
66 rue de Paris, RN14
76240 Bonsecours
4km from Rouen, RN14 direction Paris
Tel:00 33 (0) 35 80 43 11
Tariff: From FF200
Cuisine: High class Normandy style.

La Couronne
31 place du Vieux-Marché
Rouen
Located next door the
Musée Jeanne d'Arc
Tel: 00 33 (0)235 71 40 90
Tariff: From around FF150
Cuisine: Haut cuisine -
excellent. This restaurant
claims to be the oldest in
France - it is housed in
a14th century building.

L'Ecaille
26 Rampe Cauchoise
Rouen
Tel:00 33 (0)235 70 95 52
Tariff: From about FF150
Cuisine: Fish
Closed: Sun pm.

Gill
9 quai de la Bourse
Rouen
Tel: 00 33 (0)235 71 16 14
Tariff: From about FF100
Cuisine: Small restaurant
with modern decor. Menu
includes Lobster & pigeon
Closed 13-20 apr, 3-18
Aug Sun pm & Mon.

Les Nymphéas
7 rue de la Pie
Rouen
Tel:00 33 (0)235 89 26 69
Tariff: From FF165
Cuisine: French
Closed: Sun, Mon.

Pascaline
5 rue de la Poterne
Rouen
Tel:00 33 (0)2 35 89 67 44
Tariff: Buffets from FF31,
menu from FF57.
Cuisine: Bistro style

Le Petit Bec
182 rue Eau de Robec
Rouen
Tel:00 33 (0)2 35 07 63 33
Tariff: From FF72
Cuisine: Snacks e.g.
salads, quiches, pastries.
Open: 1-3pm only.

Les P'tits Parapluies
46 rue du Bourg l'Abbe
Rouen
Tel:00 33 (0)235 88 55 26
Tariff: From FF190
Cuisine: Bistro style
Closed: Sun.

How Much Can You Bring Back?

***In theory there are no limits on the amount of alcohol or tobacco for personal use.
In practice exceeding Advisory Guidelines, means you could be stopped***

Since 1st January 1993, you are permitted to bring back as much alcohol and tobacco as you like, but it must be for personal use only. So you can happily stock up for Christmas or parties or weddings.

Although H. M. Customs and Excise have no authority to limit the amount you bring back into this country they do have the right to stop you if your purchases exceed the 'Advisory Guidelines'. In this case you may be required to prove that the goods are for your own personal use.

If you are stopped, remember that the H.M. Customs officer is looking for bootleggers or those intent on resale and your co-operation will be appreciated. Other products such as mineral water, or any other non-alcoholic or food products are not limited in any way. Enjoy.

Advisory Guidelines
as set by H.M. Customs & Excise

Wine (not to exceed 60 litres of sparkling wine)	90 litres
Spirits	10 litres
Intermediate products (i.e port & sherry)	20 litres
Beer	100 litres
Cigarettes	800
Cigars	400
Tobacco	1 Kilogram

Conversion Tables

What's Your Size?
When buying clothes in France, check the conversion tables below to find out your size:

Women's Shoes

GB		FR	GB		FR
3	=	35$^1/_2$	5$^1/_2$	=	39
3$^1/_2$	=	36	6	=	39$^1/_2$
4	=	37	6$^1/_2$	=	40
4$^1/_2$	=	37$^1/_2$	7	=	40$^1/_2$
5	=	38	8	=	41$^1/_2$

Women's Dresses/Suits

GB		FR	GB		FR
8	=	36	14	=	42
10	=	38	16	=	44
12	=	40	18	=	46

Women's Blouses/Sweaters

GB		FR	GB		FR
30	=	36	36	=	42
32	=	38	38	=	44
34	=	40	40	=	46

Men's Shirts

GB		FR	GB		FR
14$^1/_2$	=	37	16	=	41
15	=	38	16$^1/_2$	=	42
15$^1/_2$	=	39/40	17	=	43

Men's Suits

GB		FR	GB		FR
36	=	46	42	=	52
38	=	48	44	=	54
40	=	50	46	=	56

Men's Shoes

GB		FR	GB		FR
7	=	40	10	=	43
8	=	41	11	=	44
9	=	42	12	=	45
			13	=	46

Weights and Measures:

Distance 1.6 km	=	1 mile
Weight 1 kg	=	2.20lbs
Liquid 4.54 litres	=	1 gallon
Liquid 1 litre	=	1.76 pints
Length 1m	=	39.37inches
Area 1sq metre	=	1.196 sq yds

Speed

kpm	mph	kpm	mph
50	31	100	62
70	43	110	68
80	50	120	75
90	56	130	81

Out and About in France

A few essential tips
to make your
travels a little easier ...

En Route:
To comply with French motoring regulations, please note what is and is not essential:

It is essential:
- To have a full UK driving licence and all motoring documents.
- To be over the age of 18 - even if you have passed your test in the UK.
- Not to exceed 90km/h in the first year after passing your test.
- To display a GB sticker or Euro number plate.
- To carry a red warning triangle.
- To wear rear seat belts if fitted.
- To affix headlamp diverters. These are widely available in motoring shops or DIY with black masking tape.

It is not essential to:
- To have a green card
- To have yellow headlights.

Parking:
Illegal parking in France can be penalised by a fine, wheel clamping or vehicle removal. Park wherever you see a white dotted line or if there are no markings at all.

There are also numerous 'pay and display' meters. (horodateurs) where small change is required to buy a ticket. The ticket should be displayed inside the car windscreen on the driver's side.

If you find a blue parking zone (zone bleue), this will be indicated by a blue line on the pavement or road and a blue signpost with a white letter P. If there is a square under the P then you have to display a cardboard disc which has various times on it. They allow up to two and a half hours parking time. The discs are available in supermarkets or petrol stations and are sometimes given away free. Ask for a **'disque de stationnement'**.

Motorways & Roads:
French motorways (autoroutes) are marked by blue and white 'A' signs. Many motorways are privately owned and outside towns a toll charge (péage) is usually payable and can be expensive. This can be paid by credit card (Visa Card, Eurocard, Mastercard), cash or even coins at automatic gates so be prepared. Contact a tourist board for the exact cost. Alternatively if you have access to the internet click on **www.autoroutes.fr.**

Roads are indicated as:

A roads -
Autoroutes - Motorways

D roads -
Routes départementales - scenic alternatives to 'A' roads.

C roads -
routes communales - country roads.

'N Roads -
routes nationales - toll free, single lane roads. Slower than 'A' roads.

Breakdown on Motorways:
If you should be unlucky enough to breakdown on the motorway and you do

---

IMPORTANT!

DRIVE ON THE RIGHT, OVERTAKE ON THE LEFT

IMPORTANT!

IF THERE ARE NO STOP SIGNS AT INTERSECTIONS, CARS MUST YIELD TO THE RIGHT

Out and About in France

not have breakdown cover, **DON'T PANIC** you can still get assistance. There are emergency telephones stationed every mile and a half on the motorway. These are directly linked to the local police station. The police are able to automatically locate you and arrange for an approved repair service to come to your aid.

Naturally there is a cost for this and fees are regulated. Expect to pay around £50 for labour plus parts and around £55 for towing.

An extra 25% supplement is also charged if you break down between 6pm and 8am and any time on Saturdays, Sundays and national holidays!

At the garage, ensure you ask for un Ordre de Réparation (repair quote) which you should sign. This specifies the exact nature of the repairs, how long it will take to repair your vehicle and, most importantly, the cost!

Emergency Phrases:

Please, help
Aidez-moi s'il vous plaît

My car has broken down
Ma voiture est en panne

I have run out of petrol
Je suis en panne d'essence

The engine is overheating
Le moteur surchauffe

There is a problem with the brakes
Il y a un problème de freins

I have a flat tyre
J'ai un pneu crevé

The battery is flat
La batterie est vide

There is a leak in the petrol tank/in the radiator
Il y a une fuite dans le réservoir d'essence/dans le radiateur

Can you send a mechanic/breakdown van?
Pouvez vous envoyer un mécanicien/une dépanneuse?

Can you tow me to a garage?
Pouvez-vous me remorquer jusqu'à un garage?

I have had an accident
J'ai eu un accident

The windscreen is shattered
Le pare-brise est cassé

Call an ambulance
Appelez une ambulance

Out and About in France

Speed Limits:
In France speed limits are shown in kilometres per hour **not** miles per hour. Always adhere to these speed limits as in France they are strictly enforced:

	MPH	km/h
Toll motorways	81	130
Dual Carriageways	69	110
Other Roads	55	90
Towns	31	50

When raining, these speed limits are reduced by 6mph on the roads and 12mph on the motorway. In fog, speed is restricted to 31mph. As well as speed traps, it is useful to know that entrance and exit times through the toll booths can be checked on your toll ticket and may be used as evidence of speeding!

Roadside Messages:
For safety's sake, it is very important to be aware of the following roadside messages:

Carrefour	Crossroad
Déviation	Diversion
Priorité à droite	
Give way to traffic on the right	

Péage	Toll
Vous n'avez pas la priorité	
	Give way
Ralentir	Slow down
Rappel	Restriction continues
Sens unique	One way
Serrez à droite/	Keep right/
à gauche	Keep left
Véhicules lents	
	Slow vehicles

Other messages:

Gravillons	Loose chippings
Chaussée Déformée	
Uneven road & temporary	
	surface
Nids de Poules	Potholes

Tyre Pressure:
It is crucial to ensure that your tyres are at the correct pressure to cater for heavy loads. Make sure you do not exceed the car's maximum carrying weight.

The following table gives a guide to how heavy typical loads are:

		Weight	
1 case of	Qty	kg	lbs
Wine	x 2	15kg	33lbs
Champagne	x12	22kg	48lbs
Beer 25cl	x 2	8kg	18lbs

Out and About in France

Traffic News:
Tune in to Autoroute FM107.7 for French traffic news in English and French.

Drink Driving:
UK drink/drive laws are mild at 80mg alcohol, compared to France. French law dictates that a 50g limit of alcohol is allowed - just 1 glass of wine. Exceeding this limit risks confiscation of your licence, impounding of the car, a prison sentence or an on-the-spot fine of anything between 200FF (£20) up to 30,000FF (£3,000!)

Filling Up:
To fill up, head for petrol stations attached to the hypermarkets (i.e. Auchan, Continent, Intermarché, E. Leclerc, PG) as these offer the best value fuel. Petrol stations on the motorway - autoroutes - tend to be the most expensive. Though sterling and travellers cheques are not accepted, credit cards usually are. Some petrol stations have automated payment facilities by credit card. These are generally 24 hour petrol stations and tend to be unmanned in the evening but do not rely on them for fuel salvation as they often do not accept international credit cards!

Currently petrol is cheaper in France - diesel is much cheaper in France.

Petrol grades are as follows:

Unleaded petrol -
l'essence sans plomb. Available in 95 & 98 grades - equates to UK premium and super grades respectively.

Leaded petrol -
l'essence or Super Graded as:
90 octane (2 star),
93 octane (3 star)
97 octane (4 star).
Gazole - Diesel Fuel
GPL - LPG (liquefied petroleum gas)

IMPORTANT!
CHILDREN UNDER 10 ARE NOT ALLOWED TO TRAVEL IN THE FRONT

Out and About in France

Caught on the Hop!

Cafés generally allow you to use their toilets for free. In shopping complexes you may require a 1FF coin to gain entry. If you see a white saucer, place a coin or two in it. In the streets you may come across the Sanisette, a white cylindrical shaped building. Insert 2FF in the slot to open the door. After use the Sanisette completely scrubs and polishes itself.

Shopping by Credit Card:

To use your credit card ensure that you have your passport handy as you may be expected to produce it.

Shopping:

Supermarket trolleys (les chariots) require a (refundable) 10 franc piece. Keep one handy to avoid queuing for change.

Shopping Hours:

Shops and supermarkets open and close as follows:

Open   9.00 am
Close lunch-time 12.00 noon
Open again   2.00 pm
Close finally 5.00-7.00 pm
Most shops are closed on Sunday and some on Monday.

Public Holidays:

Most French shops will be shut on the following days

Jan 1	New Year	Jour de l'an
Apr*	Easter Monday	Lundi de Pâques
May 1	Labour Day	Fête du Travail
May 8	Victory Day	Armistice 1945
May*	Ascension	Ascension
May*	Whitsun	Lundi de Pentecôte
July 14	Bastille Day	Fête nationale
Aug 15	Assumption	Assomption
Nov 1	All Saints'	Toussaint
Nov 11	Armistice Day	Armistice 1918
Dec 25	Christmas	Noël

*Dates change each year.

Tipping:

Tipping is widely accepted in France. However restaurant menus with the words 'servis compris' indicate that service is included but small change can be left if so desired. The following is the accepted norm for tipping:

Restaurants service usually included	Optional
Cafés service usually included	Optional
Hotels	No
Hairdressers	10F
Taxis	10F
Porters	10F
Cloakroom attendants	Small change
Toilets	Small change

Out and About in France

Phoning Home:
Phonecards (Télécartes) are widely used and available at travel centres, post offices, tobacconists and shops displaying the Télécarte sign. Coin operated payphones (becoming rare) take 1,2 & 5 FF coins. Cheap rate (50% extra time) is between 22.30hrs-08.00hrs Monday to Friday, 14.00hrs-08.00hrs Saturday, all day Sunday & public holidays.
To call the UK dial 00, at the dialling tone dial 44 followed by the phone number and omit 0 from the STD code.

Writing Home:
Post Offices (PTT) are open Monday to Friday during office hours and half day on Saturday. Smaller branches tend to close between noon and 2pm. Stamps can also be purchased from tobacconists. The cost of a postcard home is FF2.80. The small but bright yellow post boxes are easy to spot

Taxi!
It is cheaper to hail a taxi in the street or look for cab ranks indicated by the letter 'T' rather than order one by telephone. This is because a telephone requested taxi will charge for the time taken to reach you. Taxi charges are regulated. The meter must show the minimum rate on departure and the total amount (tax included) on arrival. If the taxi driver agrees that you share the taxi ride, he has the right to turn the meter back to zero at each stop showing the minimum charge again.

A tip *(pourboire)* is expected. It is customary to pay 10-15%.

No Smoking!
The French have an etiquette for everything and that includes smoking. It is forbidden to smoke in public places. However, there are quite often spaces reserved in cafés and restaurants for smokers.

Out and About in France

Money Matters:

Currency:
French currency, known as the French Franc is shown in 3 ways: FF, Fr or F. A Franc is roughly equivalent to 11p.

The French Franc is made up of 100 centimes.

Centimes have their own set of coins *(pièces)* i.e. 5, 10, 20 and 50 centimes - marked as 1/2F.

Francs are in 1, 2, 5, 10 and 20F pieces and bank notes *(billets)* are in 20, 50, 100, 200 and 500F notes.

When you are looking at a price tag, menu or receive a receipt be aware that unlike the British system of separating pounds and pence with a decimal point, in France there is no decimal point, the francs and centimes are separated by a comma

Unlimited currency may be taken into France but you must declare bank notes of 50,000 French Francs or more if your are bringing this back.

Note: The Euro became legal currency in France on January 1 1999. All prices are displayed in French Francs and Euros. The Franc will be phased out on 30 June 2002.

Currency Exchange:
Changing money from Sterling to French Francs tends to be expensive. We recommend that you use your credit card to pay for goods abroad, as credit card companies give a better rate of exchange and do not charge currency commission when buying goods abroad.

Of course you will require some cash. Change your money in the UK where it can be a little more competitive than in France.

In France you can also change money and cash travellers cheques at the Post Office (PTT), banks, stations and private bureaux de change.

Out and About in France

In hypermarket complexes there are machines available to change your Sterling to French Francs. AVOID these as they are the most expensive method for changing money. It would be better to make a purchase in the hypermarket in Sterling, as change is given in French Francs without commission charges. Although this is convenient, always be aware of the exchange rate. Some shops do take advantage.

French Franc travellers cheques can be used as cash and if you wish to turn them into cash at a French bank you will receive the face value - no commission. **Most banks in France do not accept Eurocheques any more.**

Credit Cards:
If you do choose to pay by credit card and your card has been rejected in a shop or restaurant, it could be that their card reading machine does not recognise it - some French credit cards have a 'puce', a microchip with security information on it. British cards do not have this. In this event, French tourist authorities recommend you say:

"les cartes anglaises ne sont pas des cartes à puce, mais à band magnétique. Ma carte est valable et je vous serais reconnsaissant d'en demander la confirmation auprès de votre banque ou de votre centre de traitement.'

which means

'English cards don't have an information chip, but a magnetic band. My card is valid and I would be grateful if you would confirm this with your bank or processing centre.'

If you need to contact
Barclaycard
Tel: 01604 234234
Visa
Tel: 01383 621166
Visa in France
Tel: 01 45 67 84 84

Out and About in France

Cashpoints

You can use your cashpoint card to get local currency from French cash-dispensing machines. This service is available at major banks such as:

Crédit Lyonnais,
Crédit Agricole
Crédit Mutuel

If the machine bears the same logo as that displayed on your card, such as Visa or Delta, then you can insert your card and follow the instructions. These are likely to be in English as your card will be recognised as British. Punch in your PIN and press the button marked **Envoi.** When prompted tell the machine how much you want in French Francs.

You will see phrases such as:

Tapez votre code secret - Enter your pin
Veuillez patienter - Please wait
Opération en cours - Money on its way!

Pharmacie

These are recognised by their green cross sign. The staff tend to be highly qualified so are able to give medical advice, provide first aid, and can even prescribe a range of drugs. Some drugs though are only available via a doctor's prescription (ordonnance).

Doctor

Any pharmacie will have an address of a doctor. Consultation fees are generally about £15.00. Ask for a Feuille de Soins (Statement of Treatment) if you are insured.

Medical Aid

As members of the EU, the British can get urgent medical treatment in France at reduced costs on production of a qualifying form - form E111. The E111 is available from the Department of Heath and Social Security. A refund can then be obtained in person or by post from the local Social Security Offices (Caisse Primaire d'Asurance Maladie).

Out and About in France

Passports:
Before travelling to France ensure you have a full 10 year British passport. If you are not a British National you will also require a visa and regulations vary according to your nationality. Contact the French Consulate.

Pet Passports:
Since 28 February 2000, a pilot scheme has been in force enabling cats and dogs to travel abroad without being subjected to 6 months quarantine. A blood test is required and a microchip fitted. Not more than 48 hours before return the animal must be treated for ticks and tapeworms. Only then will it be awarded the official 'pet passport'. Further information is available from PETS helpline on 0870 2411 710 or www.maf.gov.uk/animalh/quarantine.

What's The Time?
French summer starts on the last Sunday in March at 2am and ends on the last Sunday in October at 3am. Time is based on Central European Time (Greenwich Mean Time + 1 hour in winter and + 2 hours in Summer) is followed in France. This means that most of the time France is one hour ahead. The clocks are put forward 1 hour in the spring and put back 1 hour in the autumn.

Electricity:
If you wish to use any electrical appliances from the UK, you will need a Continental adapter plug (with round pins). The voltage in France is 220V similar to 240V in the UK.

Television & Video Tapes
Another important difference is that the French standard TV broadcast system is SECAM whereas in the UK it is PAL. Ordinary ideo cassettes bought in France will show only in black and white. This means that French video tapes cannot be played on British videos. Be sure to ask for the VHS PAL system.

Channel Shoppers' Drinks Tips

Tips:

More expensive wines attract higher percentages of profit leaving little room for savings - if any!

A good benchmark for a maximum spend on a bottle of wine is £10.00.

If you wish to buy wines costing more than £10.00 then the UK retailers are a better bet. This is because prices at this level are comparable and it the wine is faulty it is easier to return.

The exception is Champagne which is expensive in the UK.

The price for a bottle of wine starting life at £1.00, is made up as follows:

Cost of wine	£1.00
Duty & VAT	£1.62
Shipping	£0.17
Retailer's Profit 30%	£0.78
Total cost	£3.57

Incidentally:

UK VAT is	17.5%
French VAT is	20.6%

The big cost difference is in the duty:

UK duty on a bottle of Champagne	£1.60
UK duty on a bottle of sherry	£1.40
UK duty on a bottle of still wine	£1.44
French duty on the above products	£0.04

Incidentally:

A discrepancy:
A bottle of gin bought in the UK is 37.5% proof
In France it is 47.5% proof.

The reason:
A tax avoidance tactic by the producers. If gin sold in the UK had 47.5% proof the tax on a 70cl bottle would be £6.50 instead of £5.13. A saving of £1.37.

WANT A FREE GUIDE ?

We welcome your feedback, so feel free to contact us with your views, news and recommendations for restaurants, hotels, sights or shopping.

via our website: www.channelhoppers.net

or write to us at   19 Morley Crescent, Edgware,
                     Middlesex, HA8 8XE

Published recommendations will be rewarded with a **FREE** Channel Hopper's Guide of your choice.

Other guides in the Channel Hopper's Series:

		Available
		Available
Calais & Boulogne	£5.99	Now
Dieppe, Rouen & Le Havre	£5.99	Now
Lille	£5.99	Sept 2000
Cherbourg & Caen	£5.99	Nov 2000

Special offer £1.00 OFF:
Buy any two or more guides and get
£1.00 off each guide.

How to order:

L Cheques should be sent to the above address in favour of 'Passport Guide Publications'.

L Telephone orders welcome: 020 8905 4851

L Order on the net: **www.channelhoppers.net.**

Quick Currency Converter

FF	£@ 8.50	£@ 9.00	£@ 9.50	FF	£@ 8.50	£@ 9.00	£@ 9.50	FF	£@ 8.50	£@ 9.00	£@ 9.50
1	0.11	0.11	0.10	49	5.76	5.44	5.15	97	11.41	10.77	10.21
2	0.23	0.22	0.21	50	5.88	5.55	5.26	98	11.52	10.88	10.31
3	0.35	0.33	0.31	51	6.00	5.66	5.36	99	11.64	11.00	10.42
4	0.47	0.44	0.42	52	6.11	5.77	5.47	100	11.76	11.11	10.52
5	0.48	0.55	0.52	53	6.23	5.88	5.57	101	11.88	11.22	10.63
6	0.70	0.66	0.63	54	6.35	6.00	5.68	102	12.00	11.33	10.73
7	0.82	0.77	0.73	55	6.47	6.11	5.78	103	12.11	11.44	10.84
8	0.94	0.88	0.84	56	6.58	6.22	5.89	104	12.23	11.55	10.94
9	1.05	1.00	0.97	57	6.70	6.33	6.00	105	12.35	11.66	11.05
10	1.17	1.11	1.05	58	6.82	6.44	6.10	106	12.47	11.77	11.15
11	1.29	1.22	1.15	59	6.94	6.55	6.21	107	12.50	11.88	11.26
12	1.33	1.33	1.26	60	7.05	6.66	6.31	108	12.70	12.00	11.36
13	1.44	1.44	1.36	61	7.17	6.77	6.42	109	12.82	12.11	11.47
14	1.64	1.55	1.47	62	7.29	6.88	6.52	110	12.94	12.22	11.57
15	1.76	1.66	1.57	63	7.41	6.00	6.63	111	13.05	12.33	11.68
16	1.88	1.77	1.68	64	7.52	7.11	6.73	112	13.17	12.44	11.78
17	2.00	1.88	1.78	65	7.64	7.22	6.84	113	13.29	12.55	11.89
18	2.11	2.00	1.89	66	7.76	7.33	6.94	114	13.41	12.66	12.00
19	2.23	2.11	2.00	67	7.88	7.44	7.05	115	13.52	12.77	12.10
20	2.35	2.22	2.10	68	8.00	7.55	7.15	116	13.64	12.88	12.21
21	2.47	2.33	2.21	69	8.11	7.66	7.26	117	13.76	13.00	12.31
22	2.58	2.44	2.31	70	8.23	7.77	7.36	118	13.88	13.11	12.42
23	2.70	2.55	2.42	71	8.35	7.88	7.47	119	14.00	13.22	12.52
24	2.82	2.66	2.52	72	8.47	8.00	7.57	120	14.11	13.33	12.63
25	2.94	2.77	2.63	73	8.58	8.11	7.68	121	14.23	13.44	12.73
26	3.05	2.88	2.73	74	8.70	8.22	7.78	122	14.35	13.55	12.84
27	3.17	3.00	2.84	75	8.82	8.33	7.89	123	14.47	13.66	12.94
28	3.29	3.11	2.94	76	8.94	8.44	8.00	124	14.58	13.77	13.05
29	3.41	3.22	3.05	77	9.05	8.55	8.10	125	14.70	13.88	13.15
30	3.52	3.33	3.15	78	9.17	8.66	8.21	126	14.82	14.00	13.26
31	3.64	3.44	3.26	79	9.29	8.77	8.31	127	14.94	14.11	13.36
32	3.76	3.55	3.36	80	9.41	8.88	8.42	128	15.05	14.22	13.47
33	3.88	3.66	3.47	81	9.52	9.00	8.52	129	15.17	14.33	13.57
34	4.00	3.77	3.57	82	9.64	9.11	8.63	130	15.29	14.44	13.68
35	4.11	3.88	3.68	83	9.76	9.22	8.73	131	15.41	14.55	13.78
36	4.23	4.00	3.78	84	9.88	9.33	8.84	132	15.52	14.66	13.89
37	4.35	4.11	3.89	85	10.00	9.44	8.94	133	15.64	14.77	14.00
38	4.47	4.22	4.00	86	10.11	9.55	9.05	134	15.76	14.88	14.10
39	4.58	4.33	4.10	87	10.23	9.66	9.15	135	15.88	15.00	14.21
40	4.70	4.44	4.21	88	10.35	9.77	9.26	136	16.00	15.11	14.31
41	4.82	4.55	4.31	89	10.47	9.88	9.36	137	16.11	15.22	14.42
42	4.94	4.66	4.42	90	10.58	10.00	9.47	138	16.23	15.33	14.52
43	5.05	4.77	4.52	91	10.70	10.11	9.57	139	16.35	15.44	14.63
44	5.17	4.88	4.63	92	10.82	10.22	9.68	140	16.47	15.55	14.73
45	5.29	5.00	4.73	93	10.94	10.22	9.68	140	16.47	15.55	14.73
46	5.41	5.11	4.84	94	11.05	10.44	9.89	150	17.64	16.66	15.78
47	5.52	5.22	4.94	95	11.17	10.55	10.00	175	20.58	19.44	18.42
48	5.64	5.33	5.05	96	11.29	10.66	10.10	200	23.52	22.22	21.05